PREFACE

In the name of Allah, the Compassionate, the Merciful. All praise to be Allah, Lord of the Universe, and Peace and Prayers be upon His Final Prophet and Messenger.

For a long time, terrorism has been considered a challenge to the domestic security of societies; however terrorism being considered as a threat to global peace and security is a new phenomenon. A review of contemporary political history demonstrates that, while terrorist attacks have been frequently employed throughout history, the September 11, 2001 attacks in the United States of America resulted in an international reaction to terrorist threats. Corresponding to the United States governments' declaration of global "war against terrorism", many States have implemented counter-terrorism measures that seriously undermine international human rights values. The present study examines the impact of counter-terrorism measures on specific elements of international human rights that are at the greatest risk of abuse in light of contemporary counter-terrorism measures, including the right to life; the right to free from torture and cruel, inhuman or degrading treatment or punishment; the right to a fair trial; the right to privacy; and the right to liberty and security. Besides, for enrichment of discussions a number of cases have reviewed.

I am greatly indebted to all those who contributed in all ways to completion of this book. I would like to thank my parents Sima and Hormozdiar, and my wife Shohreh Mousavi for their great supports and helps throughout my research.

Dr. Behnam Rastegari
PhD in Public International Law
Faculty of Law
University Kebangsaan Malaysia
Kuala Lumpur, Malaysia

CONTENTS

HUMAN RIGHTS

TABLE OF CASES

Aksoy v Turkey (1996). In ECtHR.

Boumediene v Bush (2008). In United States Supreme Court.

Campbell and Hartley v United Kingdom (1990). In ECtHR.

Chahal v the United Kingdom (1996). In ECtHR.

Democratic Republic of Congo v Uganda (2005). In IACtHR.

Doorson v The Netherlands (1996). In ECtHR.

Ecer and Zeyrek v Turkey (2001). In ECtHR.

Ergi v Turkey (1998). In ECtHR.

Hamdan v Rumsfeld (2006). In United States Supreme Court.

Hamdi v Rumsfeld (2002). In United States Court of Appeals.

Islamic Republic of Iran v United States (Oil Platforms Case 2003). In ICJ.

Kadi and Al Barakaat International Foundation v Council of European Union (2008). In ECJ.

Klass and others v Federal Republic of Germany (1979). In ECtHR.

Malone v United Kingdom (1984). In ECtHR.

Moriana Hernandez Valentini de Bazzano v. Uruguay (1979). In IACtHR.

McCann and Others v United Kingdom (1995). In ECtHR.

McGuinness v Ireland (2000). In ECtHR.

McKerr v United Kingdom (2001). In ECtHR.

Nicaragua v United States (1986). In ICJ.

Rumsfeld v Padilla (2004). In United States Supreme Court.

Selcuk and Asker v Turkey (1997). In ECtHR.

Tennessee v Garner (1985). In United States Supreme Court.

United States of America v Khalid Sheikh Mohammed, et al (2008). In United States Military Commissions.

TABLE OF ABBREVIATIONS

ACHR	American Convention on Human Rights
AI	Amnesty International
ATCSA	Anti-terrorism, Crime and Security Act
CAT	Convention against Torture and other Cruel, Inhumane or Degrading or Punishment
CCR	Centre for Constitutional Rights
CERD	Committee on the Elimination of Racial Discrimination
CIA	Central Intelligence Agency
CIS	Commonwealth Independent States
CTC	Counter-Terrorism Committee
ECHR	European Convention on Human Rights
ECtHR	European Court of Human Rights
IACtHR	Inter-American Court of Human Rights
ICCPR	International Covenant on Civil and Political Rights
ICESCR	International Covenant on Economic, Social and Cultural Rights
ICJ	International Court of Justice
ICRC	International Committee of the Red Cross
IHL	International Humanitarian Law
IHRL	International Human Rights Law
IRA	Irish Republican Army
KCD	Kill- Capture Detains
MCA	Military Commission Act
OAS	Organization of American States
OPCAT	Optional Protocol to the Convention against Torture
OSCE	Organization for Security and Co-operation in Europe
PACE	Parliamentary Assembly of the Council of Europe
PATRIOT	Uniting and Straightening America by Providing Appropriate Tools Required to Intercept and Obstruct Terrorism
PKK	Workers' Party of Kurdistan
SC	Security Council
SPT	Subcommittee on Prevention of Torture

UDHR	Universal Declaration of Human Rights
UK	United Kingdom
UNCRC	United Nations Convention on the Rights of the Child
UNCHR	United Nations Commission of Human Rights
US	United States
WTC	World Trade Centre

CHAPTER I

INTRODUCTION

1.1   PREAMBLE

The history of human civilization demonstrates that terrorism is not a novel concept. Terrorist acts have occurred frequently throughout the history in different forms including assassination, hostage-taking, kidnapping and many other forms. However, the casualties were generally limited to a certain or small group of individuals. Contemporarily, terrorist acts have become an increasingly problematic issue and the international struggle against such acts has become a focal point in international relations. International terrorism, which goes beyond national boundaries, is considered to be as serious threat to the peace and security of the entire world. The use of complex financial networks; the vast efforts towards the recruitment of civilians as active members of terrorist organizations; the increasingly high financial costs of damages resulting from terrorist attacks; and the large number of victims of terrorist attacks demonstrate the complexity of international terrorist activities. Contemporary terrorists, utilizing modern tools and tactics, engage in new types of terrorism, such as bio-terrorism and nuclear-terrorism are able to cause substantial amounts of damage and cause large number of fatalities anytime or anywhere in the world.

The causes of contemporary terrorism vary. Some reasons that contribute to terrorist acts include poverty; social injustice and discrimination; poor living standards; non-adequate education; corruption; unemployment; tyranny and dictatorial governments. Other factors that contribute to the commission of terrorist acts include cultural, religious, and political factors. However, the roots of international terrorism are also much more complex than the aforementioned elements. The international community has historically largely ignored the threat of terrorism. In the contemporary world, decision makers are faced with the problematic issue of counter-terrorism and a series of legal challenges relating to anti-terrorism legislation, trials and punishment. Generally, to develop a comprehensive counter-terrorism policy, governments face an interdisciplinary issue, with unclear boundaries between the determination of friend and foe, in regard to heinous actions that have a grave impact on most of the aspects of social life and human rights.

Terrorists choose to commit terrorist acts as part of a process of rational and conscious decision-making within particular political and cultural contexts. Thus, terrorism is not, as it is often colloquially described, a kind of madness. Terrorism is a communicative act intended to influence the behaviour of one or more audiences. Terrorism fundamentally relies on symbolism and provocation. Terrorists choose targets not for their military value, but for their ability to create an extreme reaction, often fear, and their utility in prodding others to act. Many terrorists have hope that their feats will lure their enemies into self-destructive behaviour.[1] Therefore, terrorism is an extremely complex behaviour with certain motives tries to effect on audiences through its inherent violence. Terrorists are looking for the effectiveness of their acts of creation of threat and insecurity in society.

Now, it is commonly acknowledged that terrorism is not merely a domestic issue. The new face of terrorism is far more complex. A terrorist attack could occur in eastern portion of the globe, but could be perpetrated by an individual terrorist from the western portion of the globe that has been supported by a complex multinational financial network. As a result, no State is immune from terrorist threats. Therefore, counter-terrorism is recognized to require a collaborative and concerted effort by international society as whole.

The term "terrorism" stems from the French word "*terrorisme*" and from the Latin verb "*terrere*", which means "to frighten". Terrorist acts, as a means of political action, can be found throughout ancient history, as demonstrated by the tyrannicides in ancient Greece and Rome; the Zealots of Palestine; and medieval Hashashin in

---

[1] R. Law, *Terrorism: A History*, Polity Press, USA, 2009, p 3.

Iran.[2] Since ancient times, opposition groups have repeatedly utilized terrorism to obtain certain political goals. Despite considerable distinctions between ancient and contemporary societies, terrorism continues to pose a serious challenge and unsolvable dilemma for human societies.

Traditionally, terrorism and counter-terrorism studies have been highly specialized fields in political science, international relations and terrorism studies. Contemporarily, however, the academics studying terrorism and counter-terrorism represent a wide range of different disciplines, including sociology, history, psychology, theology, anthropology, criminology, law, policing studies, Islamic studies, religious studies and philosophy. Additionally, the fields of engineering, computer science and security studies increasingly focus on terrorism and counter-terrorism subjects as well. The growing range of academic perspectives enables terrorism and counter-terrorism provide rich debates that benefit greatly from a wealth of different voices and experiences that can potentially influence national and international counter-terrorism policies.[3]

Terrorism research did not begin when the nineteen hijackers simultaneously attacked the United States of America (US). It has a considerably longer history. Since the advent of international terrorism in 1968,[4] terrorist specialist researchers have searched for the root causes of terrorism in an effort to determine the most common reasons of terrorism.[5] From a scholarly perspective, terrorism is an extremely contested concept and no agreement can be found as to what the definition should include.

1.1.1   Counter-Terrorism: Human Rights at Risk

It should be emphasized that the counter terrorism as series of offensive actions to abolish terrorist activities are different from anti-terrorism actions as more defensive

---

[2] M.L Volkansec et al, *Courts and Terrorism, Nine Nations Balance Rights and Security*, Cambridge University Press, New York, 2011, pp 1-2.
[3] B. Spalek, Introducing Counter-Terrorism studies, in B. Spalek (ed.), *Counter-Terrorism: Community Base Approaches to Preventing Terror Crime*, Palgrave Macmillan, London, 2012.
[4] Attack to the "EI AI" flight 426 on July 23, 1968.
[5] M. Abrahms, The Causes of Terrorism: A Reappraisal of the Conventional Wisdom, Ph.D thesis, University of California, United States, 2009, p 3.

measures to prevent the future risks of terrorism. Normally the counter-terrorism measures apply following terrorist activities to eliminate the terrorist abilities, while the anti-terrorism employs to recognize the causes and roots of terrorism against the potential of the terrorist attacks. However, in practice despite of the differences, these two concepts are usually overlapped.

From a legal view States adopted two different policies to fight against terrorism. Some governments confine their counter-terrorism measures to the rule of law and respect for human rights; however others retaliate with widespread and systematic violations of the individual rights of terrorists as well as civilians. Committing numerous human rights abuses in the name of the "war against terrorism" has come to include extreme penalties; pervasive surveillance; and suppression of freedom by States' leaders, potentially undermining the legitimacy of government in some instances.[6]

The September 11 attacks in the US challenged both local and global security. The attacks are recognized as a turning point in the history of terrorism and serve as a warning of the potential threats to global security posed by terrorism. Nearly 3000 civilians from over 90 countries died in the attacks on the World Trade Centre (WTC) buildings and the Pentagon, which were committed by 19 hijackers. Such a massive attack had not been carried out against the US since the attack on Pearl Harbor on 7 December, 1941.[7]

Nine days after the September 11 attacks, the former US President George W. Bush announced that the US was declaring "war on terrorism". Following the investigation of the events, it was determined that the hijackers were members of Al-Qaeda, an Islamic fundamentalist terrorist organization harboured by the Taliban regime inside the borders of Afghanistan. The UN Member States condemned the attacks unanimously, however; the attacks were utilized to justify the invasion of Afghanistan by the US and its allies on 7 October 2001, relying upon controversial

---

[6] M. Y. Omelicheva, Counter-terrorism and Human Rights: Explaining Differences in the Scope and Brutality of State's Responses to Terrorism, Ph.D thesis, Purdue University, United States, 2007, p 1.
[7] A. Williams et al, *Terror Attacks*, Futura, London, 2006, pp 439-440.

international legal norms to further legitimate the military action, such as "right to self- defence".[8]

The invasion of Afghanistan was justified under the self-defence doctrine in international law by the invading countries. During the war in Afghanistan, the actions of US, UK and their allies greatly undermined international humanitarian law (IHL) and international human rights law (IHRL). The establishment of military commissions and the detention facility at Guantanamo Bay; the unknown condition of detainees, and the use of torture during the investigations of suspected terrorists are all examples of violations of rights guaranteed under IHL and IHRL during the war in Afghanistan. For example, the US justified the targeted killings operations against suspected terrorists by asserting that human rights are not applicable during armed conflicts; and that the right to life is suspended in the war time. However; the application of IHRL is not limited to peace times or non-military measures. Logically, IHRL should be applied alongside IHL protections of individual rights during an armed conflict since IHRL and IHL are complementary, rather than mutually exclusive.[9]

The impact of the September 11 attacks on international law and the law of self-defence is worrisome. In spite of the existence of controversies between States and scholars concerning the legality of the invasions, the picture was sufficiently clear. The State victim of an armed attack could react individually by invoking the principle of self-defence until the UN Security Council (SC) opted to intervene. The State aggressor could also request the assistance of other States to act in accordance with the principle of collective self-defence.[10]

The atrocities of September 11 had significant effects on international law and responses to attacks arguably undermined the authority of international law through the abuse of the international legal framework. The unilateral declaration of a "war on terrorism" by the US rises important questions regarding the exact meaning of the

---

[8] See discussion on the "Use of Force" and the "Right to Self-Defence" in Chapter IV.
[9] See discussion on the Extrajudicial Executions (Targeted Killings).
[10] A. Cassese, 'Terrorism is also Disrupting Some Crucial Legal Categories of International Law' (2001) 12(5) *European Journal of International law (EJIL)*, p 995.

phrase and whether the "war on terrorism" a real war in accordance with generally accepted definitions under international law and international legal instruments such as what exactly does this phrase means? , or is it a real war that defined within the international law and international instruments? Clear answers to these questions concerning the legality of declaration of "war against terrorism" are doubtful.

In the aftermath of the September 11, a number of governments around the world rushed to enact legislation against terrorism, or were coerced into introducing anti-terrorism legislation, as a part of the US global anti-terrorism campaign. Some States opted to resurrect draconic anti-terrorism legislative measures. While the ability of States to enact national legislative measures to combat terrorism is unquestionable under international law, such measures must not infringe or violate other rights and principles enshrined in international law. In particular, anti-terrorism laws have serious implications for human rights and individual freedoms.[11] For example the US PATRIOT Act 2001 presented very wide definitions of terrorism that consider as a risk for human rights. The UK's Anti Terrorism and Security Act 2001 negatively affected the rights of asylum seekers and refugees. Strict counter-terrorism measures undertaken by States have the potential to result in gross violations against fundamental human rights, such as the right to life; the right to freedom from torture and cruel, inhuman or degrading treatment or punishment; the right to fair trial; the right to liberty and security of the person; and the right to privacy. Furthermore, this law and similar regulations enhanced the security measures in society and negatively affect the rights of individuals enshrined within the international and regional human rights instruments.

Obviously, the duty of the governments of States is to protect their citizens against threats of terrorism that exist both inside and outside of domestic borders. Governments, therefore, must attempt to prevent and protect against terrorist threats through the use of effective counter-terrorism policies. While counter-terrorism policies could reduce the risks of terrorist activities, employing intemperate counter-terrorism measures could negatively affect the rights of individuals. In the meantime,

---

[11] C. Lumina, 'Counter Terrorism Legislation and the Protection of Human Rights: A survey of Selected International Practice' (2007) 7 (1) *African Human Rights Law Journal*, pp 36-67.

achieving a proper balance between the maintenance of security and the respect for human rights is extremely important because an appropriate balance could aid in the prevention of abuses and violations of the fundamental rights of individuals under the pretext of counter-terrorism measures by governments.

Most of the human rights violations committed under the counter-terrorism measures of States include the use of torture against suspect terrorists; extrajudicial executions; and secret, extraordinary and arbitrary detentions. For example, based on the second report of the Committee on Legal Affairs and Human Rights of the Parliamentary Assembly of the Council of Europe (PACE), a number of detainees were held in the Central Intelligence Agency (CIA) detention centres in Romania and Poland between 2002 and 2005. Moreover, this report emphasized that the detainee program gave rise to repeated and serious breaches of human rights.[12] The Committee on Legal and Human Rights of the Council of Europe, in Resolution 1562 on the existence of the secret detention centres, stated: "Such secret detention centres operated by the CIA have existed for some years in these two countries, though does not rule out the possibility that secret CIA detentions may also have occurred in other Council of Europe Member States."

In addition, the Committee emphasizes that the occurrence of "serious violation of human rights" undermine the provisions of the ECHR and the UN Convention against Torture and Other Cruel, Inhuman or Degrading Treatment or Punishment. It further reports: "The detainees were subjected to inhuman and degrading treatment, which was sometimes protracted. Certain "enhanced" interrogation methods used to fulfil the definition of torture and inhuman and degrading treatment." [13]

To abate terrorism, the world community should continue the promotion and adoption of international legal documents and legitimate responses to the threat of terrorism. The fight against terrorism requires the most powerful and affluent States

---

[12] D. Marty. 2007. Second Report of the Committee on Legal Affairs and Human Rights. *Parliamentary Assembly of the Council of Europe (PACE)*. Report on Secret detentions and illegal transfers of detainees involving Council of Europe Member States. Strasbourg: Council of Europe. p 25.

[13] D. Marty. 2007. Second Report of the Committee on Legal Affairs and Human Rights. p 6.

of the international community play a greater part in the efforts of the international community to prevent regional conflicts and secure political stability. The prevention of terrorism is often linked with the protection and promotion of human rights. This is because terrorism often thrives in an environment in which human rights are violated.[14]

The present study examines human rights law violations committed by States engaging in counter-terrorism measures; and illustrates the impacts of wrongful counter-terrorism measures on the enjoyment of human rights. The specific human rights examined include the right to life; right to freedom from torture and cruel, inhuman or degrading treatment or punishment; the right to a fair trial; the right to privacy; and the right to liberty and security. Of particular interest is the challenges faced by such rights in the context of counter-terrorism measures. For the legally enrichment of discussions several cases of the national courts and international tribunal were analyzed and scrutinized.

This book answers the important questions concerning how have human rights been violated by counter-terrorism measures? what is the appropriate law and legal framework for counter-terrorism measures? Furthermore, it investigates the potential impact of counter-terrorism measures on human rights. In the present research, human rights will specifically be addressed as one of the international legal issues in relation to terrorism. The study will explore the complex relationship between terrorism and human rights and discover the multifaceted links between the two issues. It will elaborate upon the mutual impacts of extreme counter-terrorism measures on IHRL and the positive effects of IHRL on States to respect the IHRL obligations enshrined in the international and regional human rights instruments. Above all, the current book emphasizes that the respect for human rights and the rule of law must be the cornerstone of international and national counter-terrorism measures; and suggests that the IHRL is a complementary normative framework in both law enforcement and military approaches of counter-terrorism measures, and finally stresses the IHL and IHRL together consider as legal frameworks for any State's counter-terrorism measures.

---

[14] O. Elagab et al, *International Law Documents Relating to Terrorism*, Cavendish, New York, 2007, pp xxvi-xxviii.

At the end of this research the following issues will be resolved:

i.   The link between IHRL and counter-terrorism measures.

ii.   Recognition of the IHRL as the legal framework for counter-terrorism measures.

iii.   The protective role of the IHRL for individual rights against any violation of State's counter-terrorism measures.

iv.   Violation against the specific human rights such as the right to life; right to freedom from torture and cruel, inhuman or degrading treatment or punishment; the right to a fair trial; the right to privacy; and the right to liberty and security.

CHAPTER II

HISTORY OF TERRORISM

INTRODUCTION

Undoubtedly, terrorism is representative of the dark side of human behaviour throughout recorded human history. Terrorism has always challenged the security of societies. Despite the lack of international cooperation to fight against terrorism from the middle of the 20th century, a number of international and regional treaties concerning terrorism have been ratified by members of the international community. The international collaboration regarding the form and scope of conventions has outlined different types of terrorism, but attaining a universally accepted definition of terrorism by the majority of States has yet to be achieved.

Contemporarily, terrorism is one of the major threats of our time. The military responses to terrorist activities and the wide spread restriction of civil liberties marked the first reactions to perhaps the most dramatic terrorist incident in history: the attack on the WTC on 11 September, 2001. While international and regional discussions on how to prevent terrorism in the long run are ongoing, consistent and applicable results have not yet been attained.[15]   The recent manifestations of terrorism have been described in countless books, articles, and films at all possible levels of sophistication. Terrorism is one of the most widely discussed issues of our time and also one of the least understood.[16] The extremely political nature of terrorism concept is considered as one of the most important reasons that prevent the creation of any precisely definition of terrorism by the Member States of the international society.

To prepare a legal framework for a social phenomenon and to set up a series of applicable laws and regulations, defining the issue is at the priority of importance.

---

[15] A. Zwitter, *Human Security, Law and the Prevention of Terrorism*, Routledge, New York, 2011, p 1.
[16] W. Laqueur, *A History of Terrorism*, 2001, New Jersey, Transaction Publishers, p 1.

The definition of the term is an element of the majority of scientific discussions. Definitions, by nature, assist in determining the base and characteristics of a debate. The issue of defining "terrorism" provides a starting point for debates on the issue.[17] The absence of universally comprehensive accepted definition of terrorism is more related to the inherent importance and interdisciplinary nature of such phenomena. On one hand, States are likely to accept a specific definition of terrorism according to their political tendencies and benefits. For example, the definition of terrorism contemporarily accepted by the US government is a definition based on current US policies, particularly policies adopted in accordance with the US response to terrorism after the September 11 attacks. On the other hand, terrorism is an interdisciplinary concept which means each academic definition of terrorism reflects various fields of study and present definitions from different, if not opposing, points of view. Diversity of opinions and definitions in academic level considers positive. However, the divergence between States in the international community on a proper and common definition of terrorism is considered to be a considerable barrier to cohesive international counter-terrorism policies.

Maskaliunaite opines to present a definition of terrorism depicting contemporary terrorism and the contemporary phenomena is more important than its historical provenance. The historicity of the concept remains important and informative for the overall analysis of the phenomenon, but a different strategy of assessment should be used in order to define the term.[18]

It is correct idea that defining terrorism is not merely a theoretical issue but an operational concern of the first order. Terrorism is an issue that is international in nature, rather than simply a local problem. Terrorist organizations may perpetrate attacks in various countries and the victims of the attacks can be of different nationalities. The offices, headquarters, and training camps of terrorist organizations function in various countries and the terrorist organizations receive direct and indirect assistance from different States; enlist support from different ethnic communities; and

---

[17] H.A Cooper, 'Terrorism: The Problem of Definition Revisited' (2001) 44 (6) *American Behavioural Scientist*, pp 882-883.
[18] A. Maskaliunaite, 'Defining Terrorism in the Political and Academic Discourses' (2002) 2 (8) *Baltic Defence Review*, p 7.

secure financial help throughout the world. Since terrorism is an international phenomenon, responses to terrorism must also be performed on an international scale. Developing an effective international strategy requires agreement on what specific issue is being dealt with. In other words, a definition of terrorism is necessary to formulate or enforce international agreements against terrorism.[19]

In the absence of any universally accepted definition of terrorism governments may present a wide definition of terrorism to criminalize vast number of activities in the name of terrorism. In this situation States are free to present vague domestic definition of terrorism without international surveillance of the UN related agencies.

Reviewing the history of a subject assists to better recognition of the changes and evolutions of the subject of study. In this regard, Lawrence defines historical perspective as the study of the subject in light of its earliest phase and subsequent evolution, arguing that it expands research horizons by encouraging the study of the relative stability of a phenomenon.[20] As stated by Robinson and Johns, the historical perspective is conducted as a part of doctrinal (theoretical) legal research.[21] Generally, the study of history is important because history helps to understand people and society; and provides information concerning how the society in which we live came to be.[22]

Recognition of terrorism from different perspectives and views is necessary for States to develop effective counter-terrorism policies. Terrorism has complex roots in human behaviour stemming from the historical, cultural and belief systems of a society. Therefore, a proper examination and study of terrorism throughout the history of human civilization facilitates the recognition of terrorist behaviours in society and leads to adoption of comprehensive counter-terrorism policies, which are undertaken to decrease the threat of terrorism. Obviously, application of a proper

---

[19] B. Ganor, 'Defining Terrorism: Is One Man's Terrorist Another Man's Freedom Fighter?' (2002), 3 (4), *Police Practice and Research*, p 300.
[20] B.S. Lawrence, 'Historical Perspective: Using the Past to Study the Present' (1984) 9 (2), *The Academy of Management Review*, p 307.
[21] I. Dobinson et al, Qualitative Legal Research, in M. McConville et al, *Research Methods for Law*, Edinburgh University Press, Edinburgh, 2007, p19.
[22] P. N. Stearns, 'Why Study History?' (2008) *American Historical Association*, http://www.historians.org/pubs/free/WhyStudyHistory.htm [25 January 2013].

domestic counter-terrorism policy that has been adopted based upon a comprehensive historical knowledge can facilitate reaching international consensus on a commonly accepted definition of terrorism and subsequently adoption of a unified global counter-terrorism policy.

2.2   BRIEF HISTORY OF TERRORISM

History is a hybrid discipline, combining the technical and analytical procedures of science with the imaginative and stylistic qualities of an art. There are two particularly striking aspects of the existing history of terrorism. The first relates to thematic labels, which are very important for terrorism studies to distinguish historical periods in terrorism. The second relates to technological developments and its effects in defining new episode in terrorism.[23]

Throughout political history, terrorism has been used as a pejorative term typically applied to the opposing side. While this provides a political description of the term, its significance as a legal term is more recent. The root word terror (from the Latin *terrere* - to frighten) entered Western European language lexicons through French in the 14th century and was first used in English in 1582.[24] In despotic societies, terrorism has served as the tool of enslavement and guarantor of mass obedience.[25]

To study the history of terrorism is to study the history of human civilization. Terrorism has been the cause of many monumental events of human experience and a part of the history of every country. The causes of terrorism vary over time and place.[26] . Historians of terrorism may point out that the word terror uses to the State terror of the French Revolution,[27] but they often neglect to add that, to varying degrees, the

---

[23] I. Duyvesteyn, The Role of History and Continuity in Terrorism Research, in M. Ranstrop (ed.), *Mapping Terrorism Research: State of the Art, Gaps and Future Direction*, Routledge, New York, 2007, pp 53-66.

[24] R. Young, 'Defining Terrorism: The Evolution of Terrorism as a Legal Concept in International Law and Its Influence on Definitions in Domestic Legislation' (2006) 29 (1) *Boston College International and Comparative Law Review*, p 5.

[25] G. Chaliand et al, *The history of terrorism: from antiquity to al Qaeda*, University of California Press, Berkeley, 2007, p vii.

[26] P. L. Griset et al, *'Terrorism in Perspective'*, Sage, London, 2003, p 1.

[27] 1789-1799.

phenomenon was a constant of earlier eras and has been prevalent ever since. Indeed, the aim of terrorism, which is to terrorize, is a far broader phenomenon historically than suggested by the term's current usage, which essentially utilizes it as an explanation or means of analyzing the illegitimate use of violence in terrorist-type actions.[28]

Over the last century, the character of terrorism has changed greatly. The changes have occurred not only within the methods of terrorism, but also in relation to the aims of the struggle and the character of the people involved. The popular image of terrorism eighty years ago is different than today's image, but terrorism has always engendered violent emotions and greatly divergent opinions and images.[29]

2.2.1 Schmid's Six Parts Historical Trajectory of Terrorism

Generally, Schmid divides the historical trajectory of the term terrorism in six parts. First, it was applied to the *regime de la terreur* of *Maximilien Robespierre* in the French revolution. Next, the term was applied to the anarchist and social-revolutionary bombers in the late 19th century who engaged in individual terror. The term was then applied as the world witnessed the massive "Red Terror" of Communist regimes and the Terror of the Nazi and Fascist regimes. Terrorism was then utilized to describe was certain tactics and excesses used in decolonization struggles. In the 1960s, terrorism was employed to describe certain manifestations of the Palestinian struggle and Latin American and European urban guerrilla attacks. Finally, since the 1990s, the term has been increasingly used in reference to religious fundamentalists.[30] Despite of the above extensive historical classification existing of terrorism in the human civilization in ancient time was not considered by Schmid. Therefore a long period of history was unseen to discuss.

---

[28] G. Chaliand et al, *The history of terrorism: from antiquity to al Qaeda*, pp vii-viii.
[29] W. Laqueur, *A History of Terrorism*, pp 3-5.
[30] A. P. Schmid, 'Terrorism-The Definitional Problem' (2004) 36 (2) and (3) *Case Western Reserve Journal of International Law*, p 399.

2.2.2   Three Parts Historical Review

The presence of terrorism, in any form, will discover within the following part in three different historical periods namely: the ancient times,[31] Middle Ages,[32] and the contemporary time.[33]

a) Ancient Times

Cases and stories of State repression and political violence were common in the ancient world.[34] During ancient times, tyrannicide (the killing of tyrants) was championed and honoured by the public as necessary for the greater good of the citizenry. For example, although *Aristogeiton* and *Harmodius* were executed for assassinating the tyrant Hipparchus, statues were erected to honour them.[35] In the ancient time terror was used more to destroy religious foes as a divine duty or to fight against occupation.

I.   General Situation

The origins of terrorism in ancient history were organized groups committed to systematic terrorism. The *Sicari*, an extreme Jewish faction that was active after the Roman occupation of Palestine, is considered to be one of the first groups that used terror against Roman Empire. In cultures, such as China and India, secret societies have flourished from time immemorial and their motivations were usually religious, rather than political.[36]

II.   The Assyrians

In the ancient world, the Assyrians were, perhaps, the most violent people. Faced with a dearth of resources, the Assyrians conquered those with material assets and large populations and then rolled their far, flung and diverse empire through systematic

---

[31] From beginning recorded history to the Middle Ages 5th century BC.

[32] From the 5th century to the 10th century BC.

[33] From 19th century BC until today.

[34] The Ancient time is considered the period from the beginning of recorded history until the 5th century. See, W. A. Hazen, *Everyday Life: Ancient Time*, 2006, Goodyear Book, Arizona.

[35] G. Martin, *Essentials of Terrorism: Concepts and Controversies*, Sage, California, 2011, p 27.

[36] W. Laqueur, *The New Terrorism: Fanaticism and the Arms of Mass Destruction*, 1999, Oxford University Press, New York, pp 10-12.

terror. The Assyrians are often cited as the earliest practitioners of psychological warfare. The Emperor *Assurnasirpal II* bragged of how he skinned alive impaled, burned, mutilated, blinded and decapitated the leaders and many of the citizens of the rebellious city of Susa. The Assyrians were eventually undone by their own methods in the seventh century BCE, when the burden of living under the Assyrians became so great that their native auxiliary troops revolted and neighbours toppled the empire. [37]

III. Ancient Rome

During the time of Roman Empire, the political world was rife with many cases of State terrorism. This includes the brutal suppression of Spartacus's followers after the Servile War of 73-71 B.C. and the elimination and enslavement of the Dacian nation in A.D.106. In conquered territories, Roman authority could be wielded without mercy. Conquest was often accompanied by a demonstration of terror.[38]

Political murders appear in the earliest annals of mankind. The murder of oppressive rulers continued throughout history and played an important role in the history of the Roman Empire. A number of emperors were assassinated by various persons or groups, including by the family of the emperor, the emperor's praetorian guards and the enemies of the emperor.[39]

A common form of violence during the Roman age was a regicide (the killing of King). The best-known political incident in ancient Rome was the assassination of Julius Caesar in 44 B.C. by rivals in the Senate. Other Roman emperors also shared similar fates, such as Caligula and Galba, who were killed by the Praetorian Guard in 41 and 68 C.E, respectively; Commodus, who was murdered by a paid gladiator in 193 C.E; and Caracalla, Elagabalus, and other emperors, who were either assassinated or died suspiciously.[40]

During this period of the ancient history terror and tyrannicide were common. According to historians, at that time, violent resistance to a despotic ruler was not a

---

[37] R. D. Law, *Terrorism: A History*, Polity Press, United Kingdom, pp 11- 12.
[38] G. Martin, *Understanding Terrorism, Challenges, Perspectives and Issues*, Sage Publication, United States, 2003, p 23.
[39] W. Laqueur, *The New Terrorism: Fanaticism and the Arms of Mass Destruction*, p 10.
[40] G. Martin, *Understanding Terrorism, Challenges, Perspectives and Issues*, p 4.

crime, but a civil duty. The Greek philosopher Aristotle (384-322 B.C.) presented several examples of assassinated tyrants who deserved their fates. Aristotle argued that there are two chief factors that induce men to attack tyrants: hatred and contempt. The hatred of tyrants is inevitable and contempt is also a frequent cause of their destruction. Thus, we see that most of those who have acquired power have retained their power, but those who have inherited have lost it, almost at once. In the case of the latter, living in luxurious ease, they have become contemptible and offer many opportunities to their assailants. Anger, too, must be included under hatred, and produces the same effects.[41]

b) Middle Ages to Early Modern Era

Conflicts between the Church and the State during the high middle Ages in Europe led to a new justification of tyrannicide as a justification for violence that was otherwise rejected as unacceptable. In this period the Church was the only possible universal authority tried to impose some stability and a moral compass. In theory, the Church's ideas about violence, authority and tyranny were of supreme importance.[42]

I.   Western History

From the 14th to the 18th century, during the late "Middle Ages" and the "Early Modern Era", several major developments transformed Europe and intensified interests in tyrannicide in both theory and practice. The splitting of the Western Church; and emerging ideas about popular sovereignty empowered individuals to protest their subservience to traditional authorities that were openly deemed illegitimate. Both changes provided additional justifications for tyrannicide and contributed to the modern understanding of terrorism.[43]

II.   Persian Experience

In the history of the eastern empire, one of the most important terrorist groups was the Assassins (*Hashashin*) that existed from 1090 to 1275 in Persia. The Assassins

---

[41] S. Mahan et al, *Terrorism in perspective*, Sage, United States, 2003, p 2.
[42] R. D. Law, *Terrorism: A history*, p 33.
[43] R. Law, *Terrorism: A history*, p 32.

(known also as *Ismailis-Nizari*) had political aims and their targets were government leaders. They made widespread threats against the governments in region States.

The Assassins were very adept at disguise, stealth and surprise killing. Thus, the term 'assassination' was coined to describe such tactics. They believed in the absolute righteousness of their cause and methodology. To kill or be killed was a good thing, because it was done in the name of faith and ensured a place in paradise after death. The belief in complete justification and ultimate rewards is a common belief of many modern-day terrorists. The Assassins' organization was eliminated in 1256, but they left a profound psychological mark on that era and, in many ways, on the modern era."[44] The name, or, more appropriately, misnomer, 'Assassin', was originally derived from the word *hashish*, the Arabic name for a narcotic product. The group later became known as the *Nizari Ismailis*. Finally the Assassins power lost in Alamut Mountains of Iran was eradicated by the Mongol Empire forever.[45]

III.   Great Britain

In the history of Great Britain, Guy Fawkes was a political activist who sought to destroy the Parliament Building at Westminster. Now there is a holiday for him in Great Britain. Fawkes and about other conspirators had hoped to kill King James and all other government officials who attended the opening day of Parliament. On 5 November 1605 the King's officials captured Fawkes while guarding the gunpowder. Like many terrorists throughout history, Fawkes and his colleagues justified their action in terms of religion. Like other instances of "Holy Terror", the Gunpowder Plot was deeply rooted in events that had occurred long before.[46] Until the 1700s, terrorism was widely used in conflicts, but diminished following the rise of modern nation States after the Treaty of Westphalia in 1648.

IV.   French Revolution

During the French Revolution, the word terrorism was coined in its modern context in British statements. Edmund Bruke was a philosopher who used the word to describe

---

[44] G. Martin, *Understanding Terrorism, Challenges, Perspectives and Issues*, p 17.
[45] F. Daftary, 'Introduction to The Assassins Legends: Myth of the Ismailis' (1994) *The Institute of Ismaili Studies*, p 4.
[46] G. Martin, *Essentials of Terrorism: Concepts and Controversies*, Sage, United States, p 29.

the regime *de la terreure*, commonly known in English as the "Reign of terror" (June 1793 to July 1794). The Reign of terror, led by the radical Jacobins that dominated the government, is a good example of State terrorism carried out to further the goals of a revolutionary ideology. During the period, thousands of opponents of the Jacobins dictatorship and other merely perceived to be enemies of the new Revolutionary Republic, were arrested and put on trial before a Revolutionary Tribunal. Those found guilty and to be enemies of the Republic were beheaded and executed by guillotine.[47]

French Revolution considers as the beginning of the modern development of terrorism. State-sponsored terrorism was first used for achieving the governmental targets to suppress rivals and maintain governmental power.

French Revolutionaries introduced the language and purpose of modern terrorism in the late eighteenth century, but only after seizing power. At the next several decades, radical visionaries developed elaborate justifications for using terrorism as a tool to gain power. During the second half of the nineteenth century and the first few decades of the twentieth century, some guises in terrorism appeared.[48]

V.   Anarchists and Guerilla warfare

At the late of the 19th century the Anarchists introduced "individual terrorism" as a new form of terror to overthrow the regimes, for example, the assassination of Alexander II in 1881 by Russian anarchists to bring down his monarchy. During the late 19th century and early 20th the anarchist activities led to number of assassinations in Europe and US, for instance the assassination of the Archduke Ferdinand of Austria on 28 June 1914 in Sarajevo, which led to World War I. The Soviet Revolution in 1917 led to systematic use of terror by the Communist regime in Russia to the entire society to control the population. The confrontation of the Irish against English rule in 1919 introduces terrorism to obtaining independence.

The nineteenth century, a time for great national tension and social ferment, marks the first appearance of guerrilla warfare. Guerrilla warfare appeared first during the Napoleonic Wars in Spain and Russia, then continued in various parts of Asia and

---

[47] G. Martin. *Understanding Terrorism, Challenges, Perspectives and Issues*, p 5.
[48] R. D. Law, *Terrorism: A history*, p 74.

Africa and reached its height after the Second World War within disintegrating European empires.[49]

VI.   Garrison's Summary

The Garrison's summary of the history of terrorism is divided to four periods including 18th century on French Revolution, late 19th century on anarchist terrorism in Europe and US, Early 20th century on Russian Revolution and Irish rebellion, and middle 20th century and issue of colonized countries in following table:

Periods	Origins	Types	Goals
18th century	French Revolution	State-Sponsored terrorism	Eliminate opposition, consolidate power
Late 19th and early 20th century	Europe and US	Anarchist terrorism, individual terrorism	Use of terror to bring down the government
Early 20th century	Russian Revolution	State-Sponsored terrorism	Terror to maintain power, control an entire population. Systematic society, wide use of terror
Early 20th century	Irish Rebellion	Selective terrorism	Terror to achieve independence
Middle 20th Century	Colonized countries	Terror to end colonialism	Use of selective terrorism on sympathizers and civilians

Following the French Revolution and the end of World War II, terrorism considered as a domestic issue and the organization of terror limited to a specific area of conflict. Within the late 1960's terrorism changed from local issue by domestic dimension to international stage.[50]

---

[49] W. Laqueur, *The New Terrorism: Fanaticism and the Arms of Mass Destruction*, p 12.
[50] A. H. Garrison, 'How the World Changed: A History of the Development of Terrorism', *Criminal Justice Planning Coordinator Delaware Criminal Justice Council*.

c) Contemporary Era

Reid and Chen note that Wilkinson defines contemporary terrorism as: "A form of political violence that evolved in 1960's and characterized by an increase in terrorist attacks across international boundaries."[51] The definition reflects the fact that contemporary terrorism is a form of political violence that evolved in the 1960s and is characterized by increased terrorist attacks across international boundaries, involving citizens of more than one country.[52]

Previously, distinguishing between terrorists and guerrillas; terrorists and criminal gangs, and genuine home-grown terrorism and State-sponsored terrorism was uncomplicated. Contemporarily, however, the distinctions are not as clear. Traditional terrorist movements consisted of hundreds, sometimes even thousands, of members. Contemporarily, terrorist groups can be very small, consisting of a few people or even one individual and are more difficult to detect.[53]

I. General Situation

Terrorism, as an instrument of revolutionary violence, emanated primarily from the political grievances of secular extremists prior to the events of September 11. Terrorist threats to the governments and "enemy people" usually originated in Marxist inspired ideologies, rightist reactions, and ethno-rationalist imperative idiosyncratic amalgams of these tendencies. Until the mid-1990s, religious terrorism certainly occurred, but such violence was largely a side show to the predominance of secular ideologies and ethno-nationalist tensions. This older, cold war influenced era was gradually supplanted by a newer, deadlier and primarily war, sectarian terrorist environment at first sporadically and then principally.[54]

In regards to contemporary terrorism, the occurrences of terrorism are remarkable. For instance in the wide territory of Russia, in more than 50 years, from

---

[51] E. F. Reid et al, Domain Mapping of Contemporary Terrorism Research, in H. Chen (eds.) *et al, Terrorism Informatics: Knowledge Management and Data Mining for Homeland Security,* Springer, New York, 2008, p 4.
[52] E. F. Reid, et al, 'Mapping the Contemporary Terrorism Research Domain' (2007) 65 (1) *International Journal of Human-Computer Studies,* p 43.
[53] W. Laqueur, *The New Terrorism: Fanaticism and the Arms of Mass Destruction,* p 5.
[54] G. Martin, *Understanding Terrorism, Challenges, Perspectives and Issues,* p 30.

the Russian Revolution, Tsarist Terror, Bolshevik Terror, State Terror for Collectivization of Agriculture, to Stalin Terrors, exercising of terrorism was notable. The large scale terror in China during the Mao regime, which ruled the country by killing of millions of people, is unfortunate. For example, make use of a wide range of terror during the Mao's Cultural Revolution.[55] The region of terror in China was ended by Deng Xiao-ping.[56]

II.   Scholar on Contemporary Terrorism

The majority of changes in the modus operandi and the profile of terrorists took place during the contemporary time. The meaning of terrorism change after the Second World War (1939-1945), as people revolted against European domination of the world. Nationalist groups were deemed to be terrorist groups. For instance, in India, groups that adopted violent methods against the British were branded as militant-terrorist groups. During the period between 1964 and the early 1980s, terrorism was used to describe violent left-wing groups and nationalists. In the post-Cold War era, the transnational character of terrorist groups was an advantage for terrorist groups generally. Global networking with potential allies and arms suppliers were among the opportunities.[57]

i.   Laqueur's main features of contemporary terrorism

Based on Laqueur, the main features of contemporary terrorism are as follows:

i.   Terrorism is one of the most important and dangerous problems facing mankind today.

ii.   Terrorism is a new and unprecedented phenomenon.

iii.   Terrorism is a response to injustice.

iv.   The only known means of reducing the likelihood of terrorism are a reduction of the grievances, stresses, and frustration underlying it.

---

[55] Started from 1969 and terrorized a total of 729,511 persons.

[56] N.S. Saksena, *Terrorism, History and Facets in the World and in India*, Abhinav Publications, New Delhi, 1985, pp 75-99.

[57] N.S. Jamwal, 'Counter Terrorism Strategy' (2003) 27(1) *Strategic Analysis*, p 4.

v.   Terrorists are fanatical believers driven to despair by intolerable conditions.

vi.   Terrorism can occur anywhere.

These characteristics show the importance of the novel, global and dangerous character of contemporary terrorism that is committed by terrorists. According to Laqueur's contemporary terrorism characteristics, the only way to stop terrorism is to reduce the "grievances" and "frustrations" that lead to terrorism.[58]

ii.   Shughart's three stylized waves of modern terrorism

Shughart proposes three stylized waves for the history of modern terrorism.

i.   Terrorism in the service of national liberation and ethnic separatism.

ii.   Left-wing terrorism.

iii.   Islamist terrorism.

The origin of terrorism motivated by nationalist goals, or at least that of the twentieth century's second half, can be traced to the decisions taken by the victors at the Paris Peace Conference that concluded the First World War. The left-wing terrorism roots in the 1960s and the opposition to the Vietnam War produced a wave of "New Left" terrorism as a radical group in Europe, Latin America, and the US. Shughart opines the origin of Islamist terrorism is rooted in three principal elements of Islamic history. First, the historical schism between Muslims following the death of the Prophet Mohammed and the issue of the leadership of Muslims between *Shi'a* and *Sunni*. Second, the strand of the fundamentalism woven into the Islamic theory in the eighteenth century to return back to the pure and authentic Islam of Prophet. Third, in Afghanistan following its invasion by the Soviet Union.[59]

The third wave of Shughart's modern terrorism classification on Islamic terrorism is a one sided view. Today, all Muslim countries are active members of the

---

[58] W. Laqueur, *The New Terrorism: Fanaticism and the Arms of Mass Destruction.*
[59] W. F. Shughart II, 'An analytical history of terrorism 1945-2000' (2006) 128 (1-2) *Public Choice*, pp13- 30.

international community and there is no State of war between Muslims and non-Muslim States. Based on the modern Islamic scholars Islam prohibits aggressive war and any other violence.[60]

It is a huge misconception that links the Islamic legal system to international terrorism. Today, the modern Islamic States broadly coordinate their practice in agreement with international law prohibiting acts of terrorism. In a number of instances, Islamic States have taken the lead in developing international norm in combating terrorism. Therefore, Islam or the applications of Islamic law are not the most critical elements in the presence or escalation of terrorism.[61]

The terrorism that began in the early 1990s differs from that of the 1960s and 1970s. Despite the common motives in terrorist behaviour, such as the goal of decolonization, modern terrorism stems from a mix of religious affiliation intertwined with political ideology. The frequency of terrorism attacks during this decade has been constant.[62] Some argue that there is little direct connection between, poverty, education, and participation in terrorist activities and politically motivated violence. They also mention that economic deprivation may not be associated with participation in terrorism and politically motivated violence at the individual level.[63]

III.　Summary of Period and Characteristics

There are some general attributes that have recurred with terrorist movements in different historical epochs, which allow us to make some general claims about the political and social character of terrorism. The most important of these characteristics is that terrorism rarely bursts forth spontaneously. Rather it is almost always the result of a prolonged period of increasing alienation and anger among those who perpetrated the violence.[64]

---

[60] A.G. Hamid, 'Islamic International Law and the Rights of Self-Defence of State' (2009) 2 (1) *Journal of East Asia and International Law*, p 68.

[61] J. Rehman, *Islamic State Practices, International Law and the Threat from Terrorism: A Critique of the'Clash of Civilizations' in the New World Order*, Hart Publishing, United States of America, 2005, pp 5-6.

[62] R. Young, 'Defining Terrorism: The Evolution of Terrorism as a Legal Concept in International Law and Its Influence on Definitions in Domestic Legislation', p 28.

[63] A. B. Krueger et al, 'Education, Poverty, Political Violence and Terrorism: Is There a Casual Connection?' (2002) No. w9074 *National Bureau of Economic Research Cambridge*, pp 28-29.

[64] David Write-Neville, Global Terrorism, in R. Devetak et al (ed.), *An Introduction to*

Today, the dimensions of terrorism are not limited to domestic violence, as the activities spill over onto the world's stage. International terrorism, as a new form of terrorism, is one of the best examples of asymmetrical warfare. It consists of unconventional, unexpected and unpredictable acts of political violence. International terrorism chooses targets because of their value as a symbol of international interests and the impact on global audiences. Terrorism in the international arena has been a common feature of political violence since the late 1960s.[65] In the 1990's the mean of terrorism from obtaining the advantages and gaining attention to mass destruction based on its reasons.

International Relations, Australian Perspectives, Cambridge University Press, New York, 2007, p 319.
   [65] G. Martin, *Essentials of Terrorism: Concepts and Controversies*, pp157-158.

CHAPTER III

THE BASIS OF HUMAN RIGHTS

INTRODUCTION

The protection of lives and property of individuals and the respect for human rights are two imperative issues within the civilized world. The two issues create a massive challenge for the security of human being. States have a duty to protect their citizens from the threat of any terrorist activities, while also being obligated to protect and respect human rights norms. The right to security is considered to be one of the fundamental human rights and the obligation to protect this right must be fulfilled by governments. Therefore, governments have the duty to take effective measures by employing appropriate counter-terrorism measures against terrorists. Human rights, as a protective framework for the rights of individuals, must be respected alongside the struggle against terrorism.

Stoudmann opines that lasting security and stability is not possible without respect for human rights and the rule of law. Experience has shown that conflict and instability are often caused by a deterioration of the human rights situation in the country. He gives the examples of Afghanistan and Kosovo as situations that turned into a breeding ground for terrorism. Democratic institutions, a functioning judiciary and an active civil society are necessary to address the roots of terrorism.[66]

Terrorism can impair and debilitate the foundation of social and economic development of society, and has negative impacts on the enjoyment of human rights that are emphasized in human rights instruments. Undoubtedly, the struggle against terrorism is one of the essential duties of governments in society. Governments should draw counter-terrorism measures and act effectively against the threat of terrorism. For example enacting comprehensive anti-terrorism law and regulation, refrain from providing any supports for terrorists, increase the border controls as a part of counter-

---

[66] G. Stoudmann, 'Finding a Balance between Ensuring Security and Protecting Human Rights in the Fight against Terrorism' (2002) 13 (4) *Helsinki Monitor*, p 283.

terrorism policies are emphasized through the SC Resolution 1373. However violation of human rights under the pretext of the struggle against terrorism and by the name of security via counter-terrorism measures considers as primary dilemma and difficulties to draw an effective counter-terrorism measures. The governments of the States, especially after September 11, have tightened the security of the territories through counter-terrorism measures, which led to undermining human rights. This chapter discovers applicable law and regulation as the legal framework for counter-terrorism measures.

Following the September 11, the States counter-terrorism measures were not compliant with the human rights norms, which enshrined within the international human rights instruments and human rights values outside or inside the State's borders. It is true that the terrorist acts violate human rights however; countering measures could not be used vastly as an excuse to undermine the rights of individuals. In international society where the international terrorism extensively operates in worldwide domain IHRL as an international framework protect the rights of individuals against unlawful counter-terrorism measures. International instruments are enacted to establish a system against any abuse of the rights for the peace and security of the globe. The protective mechanism of the international and regional human rights instruments is truly applicable in dealing with the danger of terrorism; therefore it is applicable in counter terrorism measures to ensure the fundamental human rights norms.

Human rights as defined by the High Commissioner for Human Rights are universal, interdependent and indivisible rights that belong to all human beings. Human rights are universal values and legal guarantees that protect individuals and groups against actions and omissions primarily by State agents that interfere with fundamental freedoms, entitlements and human dignity. The full spectrum of human rights involves respect for, and protection and fulfilment of, civil, cultural, economic, political and social rights, as well as the right to development.[67]

---

[67] Office of the United Nations High Commissioner for Human Rights (OHCHR), 'Human Rights, Terrorism and Counter-Terrorism, Factsheet, No 32, p 3 http://www.ohchr.org/Documents/Publications/Factsheet32EN.pdf [21 February 2013].

3.2   GENERAL REVIEW OF HUMAN RIGHTS

In approximately 1780 B.C, the Code of Hammurabi announced an extremely important principle: some laws are so fundamental that they apply to everyone, even the king. Such a principle is important for protecting against the arbitrary use or abuse of power. Cyrus the Great, the founder of the Persian Empire, promulgated the Charter of Cyrus around 539 B.C, which is described as the world's first charter of human rights. The clay cylinder recognizes some of the most important human rights, including social and economic rights; the freedom of movement; and religious tolerance.[68]

Persons, through membership in groups, acquired rights and responsibilities. The society's traditions and written historical documents address questions of duties, rights and responsibilities, such as the Magna Carta (1215); the English Bill of Rights (1689); the French Declaration on the Rights of Man and Citizen (1789); and the US Constitution and Bill of Rights (1791). Effort in the 19th century to prohibit the slave trade or protect the workers' rights, and minority groups was raised by the League of the Nations at the end of the First World War.[69]

3.2.1   World War II, United Nations and Human Rights Movements

The end of World War II was a milestone in the human rights movement. The idea of universal rights has subjected to number of critiques about the authority and persuasive power. The tragedy of World War II shows the weaknesses of the international system. The international system underwent a crisis of legitimacy. The modern human rights movement sought to establish minimum standards to legitimate the State's behaviour in the international community. The standards were provided through and were to be monitored and implemented by a new organization founded after World War II, the UN.[70]

---

[68] P. G. Lauren, *The Evolution of International Human Rights*, University of Pennsylvania Press, Pennsylvania, 2011, p 12.

[69] N. Flowers, ' A Short History of Human Rights', University Minnesota, Human Rights Resources Centre   http://www1.umn.edu/humanrts/edumat/hreduseries/hereandnow/Part-1/short-history.htm [10 January 2012].

[70] A. J. Langlois, 'Human Rights', in R. Devetak et al, *An Introduction to International Relations: Australian Perspectives*, Cambridge University Press, New York, 2008, p 340.

The UN Charter specifically recognizes important human rights such as the right of self-determination or non-discrimination within Article 1 (2). The UN Charter in the preamble emphasizes on the fundamental human rights and equal rights of men and women. The preamble provides: "We the people of the United Nations determined to reaffirm faith in fundamental human rights, in the dignity and worth of the human person, in the equal rights of men and women and of nations large and small."

Articles 1(1); 1(2); 1(3); 55; 56; and other UN Charter Articles place emphasis on human rights. Therefore, the UN Charter was the first international treaty after World War II emphasizing the fundamental nature of human rights, dignity and worth of persons within its provisions.

a)   Universal Declaration of Human Rights (UDHR) Six Families of Rights

After the founding of the UN, a committee was established to draft an international bill of rights, culminating in the UDHR adopted by the GA on 10 December 1948. The UDHR was a set of recommended standards rather than a binding treaty. Contemporarily, however, almost all of the norms have been incorporated in widely ratified UN human rights treaties. The UDHR proposed six families of rights as follows:

    i.   Security rights.

    ii.   Due process rights.

    iii.   Liberty rights.

    iv.   Rights of political participation.

    v.   Equality rights.

    vi.   Social rights.

The UDHR was a platform for subsequent human rights treaties; and national constitutions and bills of rights. [71]

---

[71] Stanford Encyclopedia of Philosophy, 'Human Rights', 2003, http://plato.stanford.edu/

Some rights, however, are applicable only to certain groups. Examples include the right to bear arms, women's rights, the right to manage, the rights of the child and indigenous people's rights. Not all rights claimed by people can be regarded as human rights. Human rights generally mean those rights which belong to all people, regardless of national origin, race, culture, age, sex or anything else. Such rights are universal and apply to everyone, everywhere, while more specific and circumscribed rights will only apply to certain people in specific circumstances.[72]

3.2.2 Characters of Human Rights

Donnelly identifies three main characteristics for human rights, noting that human rights are equal, inalienable and universal rights.

i.   They are equal rights meaning that all human rights are enjoyed equally by human beings, as all human beings possess the same human rights as everyone else.

ii.   They are inalienable rights meaning they are also inalienable rights that one cannot stop being human no matter how badly behaviour nor how barbarously one is treated.

iii. They are universal rights in the sense that today we consider all members of the species human beings and thus the holder of human rights

Furthermore, Donnelly defines human rights as rights that one possesses simply because one is a human being. [73]

Ignatieff argues the purpose of human rights law, is to protect humans against abuse, cruelty and oppression. Human rights protect the core of negative freedom. He mentions this is the starting point for some complex thinking about what the purpose

---

entries/rights-human [11 January 2013].
    [72] J. Ife, *Human Rights and Social Works: Towards Rights Based Practice*, Cambridge University Press, New York, 2001, p 8.
    [73] J. Donnelly, *Universal Human Rights in Theory and Practice*, Cornell University Press, United States, 2003, p 10.

and the content of evolving international human rights regime should be, however the human rights regime does not claim to be morally comprehensive. Human rights do not guarantee that anyone who is effectively protected will live a wonderful life or normally good life. Ignatieff recognizes a pragmatic purpose for human rights, which is the preparation of effective instruments to protect individuals from abuse, cruelty and oppression and degradation.[74]

3.2.3   Four Generations of Human Rights

Evans argues that taking the UDHR as starting point and conceptual framework purposed will use the word "generation" in two different inter-weave ways. In one sense, refers to historical transitions, and in another sense, refers to deepening layers or significant qualitative shift. In the field of human rights, Evans divides human rights into four following categories:

i.   The first generation: establishing principles.

ii.   The second generation: standard setting.

iii. The third generation: coping with the "new world order".

iv.   The fourth generation: making rights real.[75]

The first generation consists of the twenty year period beginning with the end of the Second World War and the founding of the UN. The UN Charter and UDHR carried the general provisions of this generation. The second generation is the fruit of what is now called "IHRL". Human rights organizations, movements, covenants and treaties were formed between the 1960s and 1980s. The International Covenant on Civil and Political Rights (ICCPR), and the International Covenant on Economic, Social and Cultural Rights (ICESCR) were adopted during the second generation. In the third generation, the end of the cold war, globalization and the September 11 attacks have created significant changes in the nature of human rights. The third generation refers to collective, environmental and developmental rights.

---

[74] M. Ignatieff, *Human Rights as Political and Idolatry*, Princeton University Press, 2001, United States, p ix.

[75] D. G. Evans, 'Human Rights: Four Generations Practice and Development', in A. Abdi et al (eds), *Education for Human Rights and Global Citizenship*, Albany: SUNY Press, 2008, pp 25-37.

Contemporarily, the international community faces the challenge of breaking the cycle of human rights violations. In the third generation the issue of responsibility for human rights, education of human rights, and accountability of human rights must be addressed. The challenge facing the fourth generation is to make the coming decade the era of implementation and making rights real.[76]

However, three categories of human rights are differently introduced by Vasak as three generations of human rights as follows:

i.   Civil and political rights.

ii.   Economic, social, and cultural rights.

iii. Solidarity rights

The first generation of civil and political rights corresponds to freedom and liberties, such as right to religion; right to speech; and the right to a fair trial. Such rights enshrined within the UDHR and the ICCPR. The second generation of human rights includes economic, social, and cultural rights. Such secondary rights include the right to social security and the right to be employed; and are enshrined within the ICESCR. The third generation consists of solidarity rights, which are collective rights that go beyond existing first and second generation rights, including rights such as the right to a healthy environment; the right to natural resources; and the right to participation in cultural heritage. Such rights have created a series of debates on individual and collective rights; and about the possibility of the full implementation of human rights that remains open until today.[77]

a) Human Rights in International and Regional Instruments

A series of the UN instruments create the core of IHRL, including the UN Charter; the UDHR;[78] the ICCPR and the ICESCR,[79] among others.[80] Besides international

---

[76] D. G. Evans, 'Human Rights: Four Generations Practice and Development', in A. Abdi et al (eds), *Education for Human Rights and Global Citizenship*, pp 25-37.

[77] P. Morales, 'UNESCO's Philosophy of "intellectual and moral solidarity" in attaining peace', Paris: UNESCO, http://www.onlineunesco.org/UNESCO%27s%20Philosophy.html [14 January 2012].

[78] Universal Declaration of Human Rights, (adopted 10 December, 1948) UNTS (UDHR).

[79] International Covenant on Economic, Social and Cultural Rights (adopted together with

activities to enact treaties on human rights, regional organizations have enacted several treaties for guaranteeing human rights, such as the European Convention for the Protection of Human Rights and Fundamental Freedoms (ECHR); American Convention on Human Rights (ACHR); the African Charter on Human and People's Rights (ACHPR);[81] and the Charter of Fundamental Rights of the European Union.[82]

I.   Specific Human Rights in the Universal Declaration of Human Rights (UDHR)

The rights emphasized within the provisions of the UDHR are as follows:

i.   The right to life, liberty and security of person.

ii.   The right to freedom from torture and degrading treatment.

iii. The right to own property.

iv.   Freedom of thought, conscience and religion.

ICCPR 16 December 1966, entered into force 23 March 1976) UNTS (ICESCR).

[80] Optional Protocol to the International Covenant on Civil and Political Rights (ICCPR-OP1), adopted 16 December 1966, entered into force on 23 March 1976; Second Optional Protocol to the International Covenant on Civil and Political Rights, aiming at the obligation of the death penalty (ICCPR-OP2), adopted 15 December 1989, entered into force 11 July 1991; International Convention on the Elimination of All Forms of Racial Discrimination (ICERD), adopted 21 December 1965, entered into force 4 January 1969; Convention on the Elimination of All Forms of Discrimination against Women (CEDAW), adopted 18 December 1979, entered into force 3 September 1981; Optional Protocol to the Convention on the Elimination of All Forms of Discrimination against Women (OP-CEDAW) , adopted 6 October 1999 and entered into force 22 December 2000; Convention against Torture and Other Cruel, Inhuman or Degrading Treatment or Punishment (CAT), adopted 10 December 1984, entered into force 26 June 1987; Optional Protocol to the Convention against Torture and Other Cruel, Inhuman or Degrading Treatment or Punishment (OP-CAT), adopted 18 December 2002 , entered into force 22 June 2006; Convention on the rights of the Child (CCRC) adopted 20 November 1989 entered into force 2 September 1990; Optional Protocol to the Convention on the rights of the Child on the sale, child prostitution and child pornography (OP-CRC-SC), adopted 25 May 2000, entered into force on 18 January 2002; International Convention on the Protection of All Migrant Workers and Members of Their Families (ICRMW), adopted 18 December 1990, entered into force 1 July 2003; International Convention for the Protection of All Persons from Enforced Disappearance (CED), adopted 20 December 2006, not yet in force; Convention on the Rights of Persons with Disabilities (CRPD), adopted 13 December 2006 and not yet in force; Optional Protocol to the Convention on the Rights of Persons with Disabilities (OP-CRPD), adopted 12 December 2006 and not yet in force.

[81] African Charter on Human and People's Rights (adopted 27 June 1981, entered into force 21 October 1986) AUTS (ACHPR).

[82] Charter of Fundamental Rights of the European Union (adopted 7 December 2000, entered into force 1 December 2009) EUTS.

   v.   The right to freedom of opinion and expression.

   vi.   The right to seek and to enjoy in other countries asylum from persecution.

   vii.   The right to education.

  viii. The right to an adequate standard of living

II.   Specific Human Rights in the International Covenant on Civil and Political Rights

The ICCPR contains of the group of individual's rights and the States duties. The rights include:

   i.   The right to life.

   ii.   The right to liberty and freedom of movement.

   iii.   The right to equality before the law.

   iv.   The right to presumption of innocence until proven guilty.

   v.   The right to be recognized as a person before the law.

   vi.   The right to privacy and protection of that privacy by law.

   vii.   The right to legal recourse when rights are violated.

  viii. Freedom of thought, conscience, and religion or belief.

   ix.   Freedom of opinion and expression.

   x.   Freedom of assembly and association.

III.   Specific Human Rights in the International Covenant on Economic, Social and Cultural Rights

The ICESCR enshrined some rights, including:

   i.   Right to work.

   ii.   Right to equal pay for equal work.

iii.   Right to equal opportunity for advancement.

iv.   Right to form and join trade unions.

v.   Right to strike.

vi.   Right to social security.

vii.   Right to special protection for the family, mothers and children.

viii.   Right to a standard of living adequate to the health and well-being of persons and their families including food, clothing and housing.

ix.   Right to education.

x.   Right to a scientific and cultural life.

Most scholars divide the sources of international law into two principal sources: conventional and customary. Of these, custom is the only universal source, generating law that is binding on all States. Conventions only create law for their signatories. Other sources are interpretative and do not directly create the law, including the decisions of national and international courts, the writing of publicists and UN resolutions. Henkins addresses the sources of human rights by introducing the new sources of human rights, namely the non-conventional sources derived from "liberal national constitutions" and *jus cogens*. Therefore, according to the Henkin's key notes, three sources of human rights could be imaginable: conventional, customary and non-conventional.[83]

3.2.4   Flexibility of Human Rights

At the outset, human rights are inalienable. Although human rights should not be denied, in specific situations, and according to due process, some rights can be restricted in the context of counter-terrorism as long as they do not undermine the

---

[83] A. D. Amato, 'Human Rights as Part of Customary International Law: A Plea for Change of Paradigms', (2010), *Northwestern University School of Law Scholarly Common*, Faculty Working Papers, Paper 88, pp 4-5 http://scholarlycommons.law.northwestern.edu/facultyworkingpa pers/88 [15 January 2013].

spirit of the right itself, such as the right to freedom of association and assembly; and the right to liberty.[84]

States are permitted to limit or suspend part of their legal obligations and restrict some rights, under certain circumstances, based on international law. Therefore, the legal recourse available to States includes limitation clauses and derogation systems codified in various treaties or through norms of customary international law. One significant difference exists between derogations and limitations. Derogations are designed to be applicable only in the exceptional case of a grave threat to the survival and national security, but limitations apply across the spectrum, from everyday public order maintenance and policing strategies to national security and military action.[85]

To use these two exceptional circumstances States have to observe special conditions according to IHRL. As above mentioned, the limitations (restriction) allowed in normal times (peace times) and derogations are applicable in time of public emergency.

a) Limitations

According to international human rights instruments, States maintain the right to limit human rights by respecting a number of conditions as prescribed by law, in pursuance of a legitimate purpose and necessity and proportionality. For example, the ICCPR permits certain limitations to enjoyment of specific rights, such as the right to freedom of expression; and the freedom to seek, receive and impart information and ideas. It provides:

> The exercise of the rights provided for in paragraph 2 of this article carries with it special duties and responsibilities. It may therefore be subject to certain restrictions, but these shall only be such as are provided by law and are necessary: (a) For respect of the rights or reputations of others; (b) For the protection of national security or of public order (ordre public), or of public health or morals.[86]

---

[84] United Nations Office of Drugs and Crime (UNODC), 'Frequently Asked Questions on International Law Aspects of Counter-Terrorism', p 97.

[85] H. J. Steiner et al, *International Human Rights in Context*, Oxford University Press, New York, 3rd Edition, 2007, p 385.

In addition, Article 8(2) of the ECHR,[87] permits limitations on the right to private and family life for the following reasons:

> There shall be no interference by a public authority with the exercise of this right except such as is in accordance with the law and is necessary in a democratic society in the interests of national security, public safety or the economic well-being of the country, for the prevention of disorder or crime, for the protection of health or morals, or for the protection of the rights and freedoms of others.

Article 9(2) of the ECHR on the freedom of thought, conscience, and religion also allows for limitations of the right, providing:

> Freedom to manifest one's religion or beliefs shall be subject only to such limitations as are prescribed by law and are necessary in a democratic society in the interests of public safety, for the protection of public order, health or morals, or for the protection of the rights and freedoms of others.

Moreover, Article 10(2) of the ECHR concerning the freedom of expression, states:

> The exercise of these freedoms, since it carries with it duties and responsibilities, may be subject to such formalities, conditions, restrictions or penalties as are prescribed by law and are necessary in a democratic society, in the interests of national security, territorial integrity or public safety, ...

Furthermore, Article 11(2) of the same convention in regards to freedom of assembly and association reads as follows:

> No restrictions shall be placed on the exercise of these rights other than such as are prescribed by law and are necessary in a democratic society in the interests of national security or public safety, for the prevention of disorder or crime, for the protection of health or morals or for the protection of the rights and freedoms of others.

Article 29 of the UDHR provides:

> Everyone shall be subject only to such limitations as are determined by law solely for the purpose of securing due recognition and respect for the rights

---

[86] Article 19 of the ICCPR.
[87] Enacted by Council of Europe on 4 November 1950 and came into force on 3 September 1953.

and freedoms of others and of meeting the just requirements of morality, public order and the general welfare in a democratic society.

In addition, Article 4 of the ICESCR states:

The State may subject such rights only to such limitations as are determined by law only in so far as this may be compatible with the nature of these rights and solely for the purpose of promoting the general welfare in a democratic society.

I. Essential Conditions for Application of Limitation

Some essential conditions for application of limitations will be elaborated in the following paragraphs.

i.   Prescribed by law

Prescription mandates that any restriction on liberties must be established by law. In another words, any limitation against incitement should take the form of a provision within legislation. The law must be adequately accessible for individuals to understand how the law limits their rights and the law must be formulated with sufficient precisions to guide individuals on how to regulate their conduct.[88]

In the context of counter-terrorism and human rights, limitations have been recognized by various guidelines, reports and documents. For example, the Council of Europe Guidelines on Human Rights and the Fight against Terrorism (2002) provides that the limitations on human rights must be defined as precisely as possible, stating as follows: "1. All measures taken by States to combat terrorism must be lawful. 2. When a measure restricts human rights, restrictions must be defined as precisely as possible and be necessary and proportionate to the aim pursued."[89]

Also, the Siracusa Principles on the Limitation and Derogation Provisions in the ICCPR, 1985, states: "Interpretative Principles Relating to Specific Limitation Clauses prescribed by law, in a democratic society, public order public health, public morals, national security, public safety, rights and freedoms of others, rights and reputations of others, restrictions on public trial."[90]

---

[88] Office of the United Nations High Commissioner for Human Rights (OHCHR), 'Human Rights, Terrorism and Counter-Terrorism, Factsheet, No 32, pp 23-25.
[89] Council of Europe, Guidelines on Human Rights and the Fight against Terrorism, (adopted 11 July 2002), p8, III http://www2.ohchr.org/english/law/ccpr.htm [16 January 2013].

Article 4 of the Human Rights Committee's General Comment 29 states:

Derogation from some Covenant obligations in emergency situations is clearly distinct from restrictions or limitations allowed even in normal times under several provisions of the Covenant. Nevertheless, the obligation to limit any derogation to those strictly required by the exigencies of the situation reflects the principle of proportionality which is common to derogation and limitation powers. Moreover, the mere fact that a permissible derogation from a specific provision may, of itself, be justified by the exigencies of the situation does not obviate the requirement that specific measures taken pursuant to the derogation must also be shown to be required by the exigencies of the situation. [91]

Guidelines of the UN Commissioner for Human Rights in Criteria for the Balancing of Human Rights Protection and the Combating of Terrorism (Commissioner's Guidelines), states as provided for by international human rights conventions, States may legitimately limit the exercise of certain rights, including the right to freedom of expression, the right to freedom of association and assembly, the right to freedom of movement and the right to respect for one's private and family life.[92]

The report of the Inter-American Commission on Human Rights on Terrorism and Human Rights examines relevant provisions to the subject of counter-terrorism and human rights, concluding that "… certain rights protected under the Inter-American human rights instruments may properly be the subject of certain restrictions that are specifically provided for in the provisions protecting these rights."[93]

ii.   In the pursuance of a legitimate purpose

---

[90] United Nations, Commission on Human Rights, Siracusa Principles on the Limitation and Derogation Provisions in the International Covenant on Civil and Political Rights, E/CN.4, 1985, paragraph 158 http://www.cidh.org/terrorism/eng/part.a.htm#B.20International%20 Human%20Rights %20Law [15 January 2013].

[91] United Nations, Human Rights Committee, General Comment 29 State of Emergency, Art 4 (2001) CCPR/C/21/Rev.1/Add.11 http://www1.umn.edu/humanrts/gencomm/hrc29.html [15 January 2013].

[92] UN Commission on Human Rights, Report of the United Nations High Commissioner for Human Rights and Follow-up to the World Conference on Human Rights, E/CN.4/2002/18 Annex 2002, Economic and Social Council, p 7.

[93] Inter-American Commission on Human Rights, Report on Terrorism and Human Rights, OEA/Ser.L/V/II.116Doc.5rev.1, 2002, Organization of American States, paragraph 53 http://www.ci dh.org/terrorism/eng/part.a.htm#B.% 20International%20Human %20Rights %20Law [15 January 2013].

The condition of pursuance of a legitimate purpose applies when the limitations help to achieve certain important goals that have already been provided by law, such as public health, public order and security of society. In other words, any limitation must be consistent with the important issues of public security and public order.

The condition of pursuance of a legitimate purpose has been accepted in a number of international and regional treaties and documents. For example, Article 19 (3) of the ICCPR, concerning the right to hold an opinion and freedom of expression, provides:

> The exercise of the rights provided for in paragraph 2 of this article carries with it special duties and responsibilities. It may therefore be subject to certain restrictions, but these shall only be such as are provided by law and are necessary.

Moreover, Article 20 provides: "1. Any propaganda for war shall be prohibited by law. 2. Any advocacy of national, racial or religious hatred that constitutes incitement to discrimination, hostility or violence shall be prohibited by law."

The Council of Europe in the Guidelines on Human Rights and the Fight against Terrorism emphasizes the prohibition of arbitrariness, stating: "All measures taken by States to fight terrorism must respect human rights and the principle of the rule of law, while excluding any form of arbitrariness, as well as any discriminatory or racist treatment ..."[94]

The Inter-American Commission on Human Rights, in the Report on Terrorism and Human Rights emphasizes that: "any restrictions must be necessary for the security of all and in accordance with the just demands of a democratic society, and that their application is proportionate and closely tailored to the legitimate objective necessitating them."[95]

---

[94] Council of Europe Guidelines on Human Rights and the Fight against Terrorism, (adopted 11 July 2002), p 8, II.

[95] Inter-American Commission on Human Rights, Report on Terrorism and Human Rights, OEA/Ser.L/V/II.116Doc.5rev.1, 2002, Organization of American States, paragraph 55.

In addition, the Siracusa Principles on the Limitation and Derogation Provisions in the ICCPR states that the laws that force limitations on enjoyment of human rights must be reasonable, clear and accessible to everyone, providing:

> 15. No limitation on the exercise of human rights shall be made unless provided for by national law of general application which is consistent with the Covenant and is in force at the time the limitation is applied. 16. Laws imposing limitations on the exercise of human rights shall not be arbitrary or unreasonable. 17. Legal rules limiting the exercise of human rights shall be clear and accessible to everyone. 18. Adequate safeguards and effective remedies shall be provided by law against illegal or abusive imposition or application of limitations on human rights.[96]

iii.   Necessity and proportionality

The condition of necessity and proportionality is an additional safeguard that requires States to ensure that limitations do not impair democratic functions of society. Countering terrorism permits the limitations of certain rights. Such limitation, however, must be necessary to achieve a particular counter-terrorism objective and to be necessary the exits of a rational link between the limiting measures and pursuit of certain goals. The provisions and the manner of limitations must also be proportional to the importance of the objective being pursued.[97]

Such conditions have been approved in a number of human rights instruments and documents, such as Article 19 of the ICCPR. The Council of Europe, in the Guidelines on Human Rights and the Fight against Terrorism, emphasizes on this condition and provides: "2. When a measure restricts human rights, restrictions must be defined as precisely as possible and be necessary and proportionate to the aim pursued."[98]

Furthermore, the Inter-American Commission on Human Rights, in the Report on Terrorism and Human Rights, stated: "any restrictions must be necessary for the

---

[96] United Nations, Commission on Human Rights, Siracusa Principles on the Limitation and Derogation Provisions in the International Covenant on Civil and Political Rights, E/CN.4 1985, paragraphs 15-18.

[97] Office of the United Nations High Commissioner for Human Rights (OHCHR), 'Human Rights, Terrorism and Counter-Terrorism, Factsheet, No 32, pp 25-26.

[98] Council of Europe Guidelines on Human Rights and the Fight against Terrorism, (adopted 11 July 2002), p 8, III.

security of all and in accordance with the just demands of a democratic society, and that their application be proportionate and closely tailored to the legitimate objective necessitating them."[99]

The Siracusa Principles emphasize the "necessity of limitations" on the Limitation and Derogation Provisions in the ICCPR, providing:

> 10. Whenever a limitation is required in the terms of the Covenant to be "necessary", this term implies that the limitation: (a) is based on one of the grounds justifying limitations recognized by the relevant article of the Covenant, (b) responds to a pressing public or social need, (c) pursues a legitimate aim, and (d) is proportionate to that aim.[100]

b) Derogations

Derogation means that in certain circumstances, such as armed conflicts or public emergency, States are permitted to derogate from specific rights. The consistency of adopted counter-terrorism measures with international legal obligations, such as IHL and peremptory norms of international law, is essential. Article 4(1) of the ICCPR sets out the requirements of derogation of certain rights by Members States, which must occur in a time of public emergency and threatens the existence of the State.[101] The Article provides:

> In time of public emergency which threatens the life of the nation and the existence of which is officially proclaimed, the States Parties to the present Covenant may take measures derogating from their obligations under the present Covenant to the extent strictly required by the exigencies of the situation, provided that such measures are not inconsistent with their other obligations under international law and do not involve discrimination solely on the ground of race, colour, sex, language, religion or social origin.

In addition, Article 15(1) of the ECHR provides:

---

[99] Inter-American Commission on Human Rights, Report on Terrorism and Human Rights, OEA/Ser.L/V/II.116Doc.5rev.1, 2002, Organization of American States, Paragraphs53 and 55.

[100] United Nations, Commission on Human Rights, Siracusa Principles on the Limitation and Derogation Provisions in the International Covenant on Civil and Political Rights, E/CN.4 1985, paragraph 10.

[101] International Covenant on Civil and Political Rights (adopted 16 December 1966, entered into force 23 March 1976) UNTS (ICCPR) Art 4 (1).

> In time of war or other public emergency threatening the life of the nation any High Contracting Party may take measures derogating from its obligations under this Convention to the extent strictly required by the exigencies of the situation, provided that such measures are not inconsistent with its other obligations under international law. [102]

Additionally, Article 27(1) of the OAS permits derogation of certain rights, providing:

> In time of war, public danger, or other emergency that threatens the independence or security of a State Party, it may take measures derogating from its obligations under the present Convention to the extent and for the period of time strictly required by the exigencies of the situation…[103]

The Human Rights Committee, in General Comment 29, emphasizes that the ability to derogate occurs only in a time of public emergency, which threatens the existence of the State, stating:

> The Covenant requires that even during an armed conflict measures derogating from the Covenant are allowed only if and to the extent that the situation constitutes a threat to the life of the nation. If States parties consider invoking Article 4 in other situations than an armed conflict, they should carefully consider the justification and why such a measure is necessary and legitimate in the circumstances.[104]

Derogation concerns the possibility of the suspension of specific rights and, as illustrated by Lehmann, is not the equivalent to the abrogation and abolition of a right. Furthermore, derogation clauses do not suspend the rule of law. International law leaves no place for the suspension of the rule of law and general principles of international law remain applicable in cases of derogation.[105]

Article 15 of the ECHR identifies four criteria for determining whether a situation amounts to a time of public emergency that threatens the existence of the State:

---

[102] European Convention for the Protection of Human Rights and Fundamental Freedoms (adopted 4 November 1950, entered into force 3 September 1953) EUTS (ECHR).

[103] American Convention on Human Rights (adopted 22 November 1969, entered 18 July 1978) OASTS (ACHR) Art 27(1).

[104] United Nations, Human Rights Committee, General Comment 29 State of Emergency, paragraph 3 (2001) CCPR/C/21/Rev.1/Add.11.

[105] J. M. Lehmann, 'Limits to Counter-Terrorism: Comparing Derogation from the International Covenant on Civil and Political Rights and the European Convention on Human Rights', p 104 http://projects.essex.ac.uk/ehrr/V8N1/Lehmann.pdf [08 October 2012].

i.   It should be a crisis or emergency that is actual or imminent.

ii.   It must be exceptional, such that "normal" measures are inadequate.

iii.   It must threaten the continuance of the organized life of the community.

iv.   It must affect the entire population of the State taking measures.[106]

According to Article 4(3) of the ICCPR, the derogating State Party must immediately inform other States Parties for the reasons of derogation, stating that:

> Any State Party to the present Covenant availing itself of the right of derogation shall immediately inform the other States Parties to the present Covenant, through the intermediary of the Secretary-General of the United Nations, of the provisions from which it has derogated and of the reasons by which it was actuated.

Based on the aforementioned Article and provision of the Article 4 (1) of the ICCPR, the duration of derogation is temporary and must strictly comply with the principles of the necessity and proportionality.[107] The Human Right Committee, in General Comment 29, states:

> Derogation from some Covenant obligations in emergency situations is clearly distinct from restrictions or limitations allowed even in normal times under several provisions of the Covenant. Nevertheless, the obligation to limit any derogation to those strictly required by the exigencies of the situation reflects the principle of proportionality which is common to derogation and limitation powers. ...When considering States Parties' reports the Committee has expressed its concern over insufficient attention being paid to the principle of proportionality.

3.2.5   Classification of the Rights

Rights can be divided into derogable and non-derogable rights, but some non-derogable rights may be restricted. All absolute rights are perceived as non-derogable. According to the ICCPR, no derogation is possible for Articles 6, 7, 8, 11, 15, 16, and 18, which concern the right to life;[108] prohibition on torture, cruel, inhuman or

---

[106] A. Conte, *Hand Book on Human Rights Compliance While Countering Terrorism*, Centre on Global Counter-Terrorism Cooperation, 2008, p 13 http://www.globalct.org/images/content /pdf/reports/human_rights_handbook.pdf [03 October 2012].

[107] United Nations, Human Rights Committee, General Comment 29 State of Emergency, paragraph 4 (2001) CCPR/C/21/Rev.1/Add.11.

degrading treatment or punishment;[109] prohibition on slavery and servitude;[110] prohibition of imprisonment for contractual obligation;[111] prohibition on retrospective criminal punishments;[112] right to recognition as a person before the law;[113] and right to freedom of thought, conscience and religion,[114] respectively.

a) Conte's Classification of the Rights

Conte classifies human rights into four categories:

    i.   The right which is a peremptory norm of customary international law.

    ii.   The rights those are non-derogable under applicable human rights treaties.

    iii.   The rights those are only derogable during a state of emergency threatening the life of the nations.

    iv.   The rights that fall outside one the three latter categories.[115]

I. Peremptory Norm of Customary International Law (*Jus Cogens*)

Article 53 of the Vienna Convention on the Law of Treaties 1969, concerning treaties conflicting with a peremptory norm of general international law (*jus cogens*), defines a peremptory norm of general international law as a non-derogable right that can be modified only by a subsequent norm of general international law of the same character.[116] For example, the *jus cogens* prohibition against torture cannot be restricted.

The Human Rights Committee maintains that the rights and freedoms available under customary international law, which are applicable to all States, may

---

[108] International Covenant on Civil and Political Rights (ICCPR), Art 6.
[109] ICCPR, Art 7.
[110] ICCPR, Art 8.
[111] ICCPR, Art 11.
[112] ICCPR, Art 15.
[113] ICCPR, Art 16.
[114] ICCPR, Art 18.
[115] A. Conte, *Hand Book on Human Rights Compliance While Countering Terrorism*, p 9.
[116] See, Article 53 of the Vienna Convention on the Law of Treaties 1969; and the ICJ's advisory opinion on Reservations to the Convention on the Prevention and Punishment of Genocide, 1951 ICJ Rep. 15 (May 28).

not be derogable even if not listed in Article 4(2) of the ICCPR. General Comment 29 states as follows:

> Despite this right, prescribed in article 10 of the Covenant, is not separately mentioned in the list of non-derogable rights in article 4, paragraph 2, the Committee believes that here the Covenant expresses a norm of general international law not subject to derogation. This is supported by the reference to the inherent dignity of the human person in the preamble to the Covenant and by the close connection between articles 7 and 10. ...[117]

Moreover, the Human Rights Committee stated:

> It is inherent in the protection of rights explicitly recognized as non-derogable in article 4, paragraph 2, that they must be secured by procedural guarantees, including, often, judicial guarantees. The provisions of the Covenant relating to procedural safeguards may never be made subject to measures that would circumvent the protection of non-derogable rights. [118]

Additionally, the Inter-American Court of Human Rights (IACtHR) considers the procedural safeguards as non-derogable rights, stating:

> The Court must also observe that the Constitutions and legal systems of the States Parties that authorize, expressly or by implication, the suspension of the legal remedies of *hábeas corpus* or of "amparo" in emergency situations cannot be deemed to be compatible with the international obligations imposed on these States by the Convention. [119]

II. Non-Derogable Rights

Non-derogable rights are prohibited rights that set out in the human rights treaties. The ICCPR establishes several non-derogable rights within its provisions, including:

i.   Right to life;[120]

ii. Protection from torture or cruel, inhuman, or degrading treatment or punishment;[121]

---

[117] United Nations, Human Rights Committee, General Comment 29 State of Emergency, paragraph 4 (2001) CCPR/C/21/Rev.1/Add.11, paragraph 13.

[118] United Nations, Human Rights Committee, General Comment 29 State of Emergency, paragraph 4 (2001) CCPR/C/21/Rev.1/Add.11, paragraph 15.

[119] Inter-American Court of Human Rights, Advisory Opinion OC-8/87 on *habeas corpus* in emergency situations, 30 January 1987, paragraphs 42, 43.

[120] ICCPR, Art 6: "1. Every human being has the inherent right to life. This right shall be protected by law. No one shall be arbitrarily deprived of his life."

[121] ICCPR, Art 7: "No one shall be subjected to torture or to cruel, inhuman or degrading

iii.   Protection from slavery and servitude;[122]

iv.   Protection from imprisonment for failure to fulfill a contract;[123]

v.   Protection from retrospective penalties;[124]

vi.   Right to be recognized as a person before the law;[125]

vii.   Freedom of thought, conscience, and religion.[126]

Conte illustrates that non-derogable rights may, in certain circumstances, be capable of limitation depending on particular expression of the right, but peremptory rights may not be limited at all. For example, the Human Rights Committee explains that limitations and restrictions cannot be justified such as freedom of manifest one's religion or belief, stating: "Even in times of most serious public emergencies, States that interfere with the freedom to manifest one's religion or belief must justify their actions by referring to the requirements specified in article 18, paragraph 3." [127] Such limitations must be both necessary and proportionate to the exigencies of situation.[128]

III. Derogable Rights only in States of Emergency

State of emergency means the situation that States can derogate some rights during specific period of time. For example, Article 15 of the ECHR provides: "In time of war or other public emergency threatening the life of the nation any High Contracting Party may take measures derogating from its obligations."[129]

---

treatment or punishment. In particular, no one shall be subjected without his free consent to medical or scientific experimentation."

[122] ICCPR, Art 8(1) and (2) "1. No one shall be held in slavery; slavery and the slave-trade in all their forms shall be prohibited. 2. No one shall be held in servitude."

[123] ICCPR, Art 11 of the: "No one shall be imprisoned merely on the ground of inability to fulfill a contractual obligation."

[124] ICCPR, Art 15: "1. No one shall be held guilty of any criminal offence on account of any act or omission which did not constitute a criminal offence, under national or international law, at the time when it was committed. Nor shall a heavier penalty be imposed than the one that was applicable at the time when the criminal offence was committed. If, subsequent to the commission of the offence, provision is made by law for the imposition of the lighter penalty, the offender shall benefit thereby."

[125] ICCPR, Art 16: "Everyone shall have the right to recognition everywhere as a person before the law."

[126] ICCPR, Art 18(1): "1. Everyone shall have the right to freedom of thought, conscience and religion."

[127] United Nations, Human Rights Committee, General Comment 29 State of Emergency, paragraph 4 (2001) CCPR/C/21/Rev.1/Add.11, paragraph 7.

[128] A. Conte, *Hand Book on Human Rights Compliance While Countering Terrorism*, p 12.

[129] European Convention on Human Rights (ECHR).

The ECtHR identified four criteria to determine according to Article 15 of the ECHR, "a time of public emergency with threatens life of the nation":

i.   It should be a crisis or emergency that is actual or imminent;

ii.   It must be exceptional, such that normal measures are inadequate;

iii. It must threaten the continuance of the organized life of the community; and

iv.   It must effect the entire population of the State takes measures.[130]

Moreover, in regards to time of public emergency "which threatens the life of the nation", Article 4 of the ICCPR provides:

> States Parties to the present Covenant may take measures derogating from their obligations under the present Covenant to the extent strictly required by the exigencies of the situation, provided that such measures are not inconsistent with their other obligations under international law and do not involve discrimination solely on the ground of race, colour, sex, language, religion or social origin.

In addition, paragraph 4 General Comment 29 of the Human Rights Committee, provides:

> Derogation from some Covenant obligations in emergency situations is clearly distinct from restrictions or limitations allowed even in normal times under several provisions of the Covenant. Nevertheless, the obligation to limit any derogation to those strictly required by the exigencies of the situation reflects the principle of proportionality which is common to derogation and limitation powers.

Also, Article 27 of the ACHR consists of provisions in the subject of time of emergency, however this provision contrast with the ECHR and ICCPR use the clause "threatens the independence or security of a State" instead of "threatens the life of the nation" as the essential condition, which permits a State to simply derogate from its obligations to protect such rights. Article 27 states:

> In time of war, public danger, or other emergency that threatens the independence or security of a State Party, it may take measures derogating

---

[130] A. Conte, *Hand Book on Human Rights Compliance While Countering Terrorism*, p 13.

from its obligations under the present Convention to the extent and for the period of time strictly required by the exigencies of the situation, provided that such measures are not inconsistent with its other obligations under international law and do not involve discrimination on the ground of race, color, sex, language, religion, or social origin.

IV. The Rights outside the Category (Other rights)

'Other rights' are rights which are not peremptory, non-derogable or subject to limitation in time of emergency. The limitation of these rights is allowed even in time of peace under various provisions of the ICCPR, but the limitation must be prescribed by law; necessary and proportionate; and non-discriminatory.[131] The Human Right Committee has acknowledged that the limitation of rights is allowed even in time of peace under various provisions of the ICCPR,[132] such as the right to freedom of association[133] and the right to peaceful assembly.[134]

CHAPTER IV

COUNTER-TERRORISM AND INTERNATIONAL HUMAN RIGHTS

4.1   INTRODUCTION

Within the conventional sources of human rights (regional and international human rights instruments); no specific provisions concerning the prohibition of terrorism

---

[131] See discussions on "Flexibility of Human Rights" in Chapter V.
[132] A. Conte, pp 15-16.
[133] ICCPR, Art 22.
[134] ICCPR, Art 21.

exist. IHRL treaties do not use the term "terrorism" in a context-specific sense. The IHRL treaties do not require States to criminalize specific human rights violations in their national law. IHRL is not the source of States' duties to criminalize terrorist violence. The duty of States to repress and fight against terrorism are derived from the subject-specific terrorism conventions;[135] and GA[136] and SC Resolutions,[137] rather than from IHRL provisions. [138]

Terrorism directly undermines the content of the UN Charter in regards to fundamental human rights and dignity and worth of individuals; the rule of law; peaceful resolution of conflicts; protection of civilians; security of the people; and peaceful relation between States mentioned in preamble of the Charter. The impact of terrorism on human rights and the necessity of counter-terrorism measures to comply with human rights obligations has been recognized by the SC and GA; and international anti-terrorism conventions. For example, SC Resolutions 1456, 2003 provides: "States must ensure that any measure taken to combat terrorism comply with all their obligations under international law, and should adopt such measures in accordance with international law, in particular international human rights, refugee, and humanitarian law." Furthermore, the SC Resolution 1624, 2005 and GA Resolution 57/219, 2003 emphasize on fighting against tall forms of terrorism with similar phrases.

In addition for example Resolution 60/158 2005 states:

> ... measures taken at all levels against terrorism, consistent with international law, in particular international human rights law and refugee and humanitarian law, to the functioning of democratic institutions and the maintenance of peace and security and thereby to the full enjoyment of human rights, as well as the need to continue this fight, including through international cooperation and the strengthening of the role of the United Nations in this respect. ...

---

[135] For example: Articles 15, 17, and 21 of the International Convention for the Suppression of the Financing of Terrorism.

[136] For example: Res.54/110 (1999), Res.60/288 (2006), Res.63/185 (2008), Res. 64/38 (2010), Res.66/171 (2011), and Res. 66/178 (2011).

[137] For example: Resolutions 1267, 1269, 1368, and 1373.

[138] E. Stubbins Batesand et al, *Terrorism and International Law, Accountability, Remedies, and Reforms*, 2011, Oxford University Press, New York, p 82.

In addition the GA within the Resolution 60/288 emphasizes the observation of the UN Charter and its obligations alongside IHRL, refugee law and IHL while combating terrorism.

Article 15 of the International Convention for the Suppression of Financing of Terrorism emphasizes on the equality of persons in prosecuting or punishing. Furthermore, Article 17 highlights the observation of all human rights of the person who is taken into custody "including enjoyment of all rights and guarantees" in conformity with the States laws and the IHRL. Moreover, Article 21 emphasizes the responsibility of States and individuals under international law and purposes of the UN Charter and "other relevant conventions".

Within the similar phrases to Article 17 of the International Convention for the Suppression of Financing of Terrorism the International Convention for the Suppression of Acts of Nuclear Terrorism guarantees the rights of the accused person for the acts of terrorist activities in the contents of Article 12.

On the human rights agenda, terrorism is not a new issue. For many years, acts of terrorism in all forms have endangered and killed innocent people; jeopardized fundamental freedoms; and impaired the dignity of human beings. States are obligated to take measures to protect the fundamental rights against terrorist acts.[139] The following discussions will deal with the issue of the link between counter-terrorism and the IHRL.

Terrorism and human rights link together from two ways namely the rights of victims of terrorist acts and the rights of accused persons to terrorist activities (actors).On one hand, terrorism has a direct impact on human rights by jeopardizing the right to life and physical integrity of terrorist attack victims. Another important issue in relation to the human rights and terrorism is the support of the victims of terrorist incidents. GA Resolutions 60/1 October 2005 and 60/288 September 2006 (The UN Global Counter-Terrorism Strategy) emphasize assisting the victims of

---

[139] S. von Schorlemer, 'Human Rights: Substantive and Institutional Implications of the War against Terrorism' (2003) 14 (2) *European Journal of International Law (EJIL)*, p 265.

terrorism and their families, with the latter resolution recommending the establishment of national systems of assistance.

Resolution 60/288 on the "UN Global Counter-Terrorism Strategy" further emphasizes assisting States to develop such national systems; striving to promote international solidarity in support of victims; and fostering the involvement of civil society in a global campaign against terrorism and its condemnation. This could include the GA exploring the possibility of developing practical mechanisms to provide assistance to victims.

On the other hand, the IHRL and human rights instruments govern the responsibilities of States for violations involving the working of private security companies on behalf of the State; inadequate criminal legislations to govern the terrorist activities; and failure to act to prevent the terrorist groups' activities in the territory of a State.[140] Counter-terrorism is a series of policies and measures carried out by international or State agencies to prevent terrorist acts. The counter-terrorism measures are not limited to actions taken inside State borders as they often involve policies, measures, and offensive and defensive actions elsewhere in the international community.

4.1.1   United Nations, Human Rights and Counter-Terrorism

Historically, there are three distinct periods of UN counter-terrorism activities relevant to human rights inquiry. These periods are from 1972 to 1993, from 1993 to 2001, and post- September 11. Prior to 1972, the UN primarily focused on the safety of aircrafts. The first stage of significant UN interest in terrorism began in response to the kidnapping and the massacre of Israeli athletes at the Munich Olympics in 1972. The second period of UN counter-terrorist activity resulted from the remarkable world conference on human rights that took place in 1993 and produced the Vienna Declaration and Program of Action (Vienna Declaration). The third period of U.N. counter-terrorism activity resulted from the September 11 attacks that occurred in the US.[141]

---

[140] United Nations Office of Drugs and Crime (UNODC), 'Frequently Asked Questions on International Law Aspects of Counter-Terrorism', pp 91-92.

a) United Nations Secretary General Statements: Protection of Human Rights while Countering Terrorism

As the terrorism considers a grave violation of human rights any prevention of terrorism in any counter-terrorism approaches must undertake to ensure respect for human rights norms. Former UN Secretary General Kofi Annan, in his statement to the Security Council on 18 January 2002, mentioned that:

> We should all be clear that there is no trade-off between effective action against terrorism and the protection of human rights. On the contrary, I believe that in the long term we shall find that human rights, along with democracy and social justice, are one of the best prophylactics against terrorism.[142]

In addition he has emphasized on three essential rules to countering terrorism. He stated:

> Terrorist acts constitute grave violations of human rights. Our responses to terrorism, as well as our efforts to thwart it and prevent it should uphold the human rights that terrorists aim to destroy. Human rights, fundamental freedoms and the rule of law are essential tools in the effort to combat terrorism-not privileges to be sacrificed at a time of tension.[143]

b) United Nations Commission on Human Rights

Since 1985, the Sub-Commission on the Promotion and Protection of Human Rights has appointed a human rights and counter-terrorism expert. In 2005, a UN Special Rapporteur on the Promotion and Protection of Human Rights while Countering Terrorism was appointed for a three year term. Following the September 11 attacks, the GA and Commission on Human Rights explicitly called upon the relevant UN human rights mechanisms to consider, within their mandates, the protection of human rights and fundamental freedoms in the context of measures to combat terrorism. Since the Human Rights Council came into being in June 2006, it has endorsed the approach of the now defunct Commission for Human Rights in these respects.[144]

---

[141] M. D. Kielsgard, 'A Human Rights Approach to Counter-Terrorism', pp 273-276.

[142] The UN Secretary General Kofi Annan statement to the Security Council on 18 January 2002, accessible at: http://www.un.org/News/Press/docs/2002/sgsm8105.doc.htm [25 September 2012].

[143] The Secretary General, All Must Work Together to Counter Terrorism, Prevent Spread of Weapons of Mass Destruction, Press Release, (06/03/2003), U.N. Doc. SG/SM/8624-SC/7680 http://www.un.org/News/Press/docs/2003/sgsm8624.doc.htm [07 April 2013].

[144] Organization for Security and Co-operation in Europe (OSCE), *Countering Terrorism,*

Moreover, the Commission on Human Rights stated in paragraphs three, four and five of the Resolution 2004/87:

> Reaffirming also the fundamental importance, including in response to terrorism and the fear of terrorism, of respecting all human rights and fundamental freedoms and the rule of law, Recalling that States are under the obligation to protect all human rights and fundamental freedoms of all persons, Recognizing that the respect for human rights, democracy and the rule of law are interrelated and mutually reinforcing.

c) Security Council and General Assembly Resolutions: Protection of Human Rights while Countering Terrorism

The UN through the adoption of a number of Resolutions has taken remarkable practical steps to protect human rights in counter-terrorism. The High Commissioner for Human Rights, pursuant to GA Resolution 48/141, 1993 that decided to "create the post of the High Commissioner for Human Rights", emphasized the importance of the promotion and protection of human rights in effective counter-terrorism strategies, stating:

> Counter-terrorism strategies pursued before and after 11 September have sometimes undermined efforts to enhance respect for shared human rights values. Excessive measures have been taken in several parts of the world that suppress or restrict individual rights including privacy rights, freedom of thought, presumption of innocence, fair trial, the right to seek asylum, political participation, freedom of expression and peaceful assembly.[145]

d) Four Pillars of Action to the Global Counter-Terrorism Strategy

The UN, through the adoption of GA Resolution 60/288 an annex Plan of Action of September 2006, enhanced international, national and regional efforts to counter-terrorism. In September 2008, in GA Resolution 62/272, the Member States reaffirmed their commitment to the "Global Counter-Terrorism Strategy" and pledged to straighten their efforts to implement it. The Strategy rests on four pillars of action:

Protecting Human Rights: A Manual, 2007, OSCE Office for Democratic Institutions and Human Rights (ODIHR), Poland, p 37 http://www.osce.org/odihr/29103 [1 March 2013].

[145] UN Commission on Human Rights, 27 February 2002, Report of the United Nations High Commissioner for Human Rights submitted pursuant to General Assembly resolution 48/141, 'Human Rights: A Uniting Framework', Economic and Social Council, paragraph 9 http://www.unhchr.ch/Huri docda/Huridoca.nsf/0/817eec31cd2810f9c1256b870058a3e5/$FILE/G0211021.pdf [20 February 2013].

i.   Measures to address the conditions conducive to the spread of terrorism.

ii.   Measures to prevent and combat terrorism.

iii. Measures to build state capacity to prevent and combat terrorism and to strengthen the role of the United Nations system in that regard.

iv.   Measures to ensure respect for human rights for all and the rule of law as the fundamental basis for the fight against terrorism.[146]

For the first time, all UN Member States have agreed to a common strategic approach to fighting terrorism, not only sending a clear message that terrorism is unacceptable in all its forms and manifestations; but also resolving to take practical steps, individually and collectively, to ensure that human rights and the rule of law are part of the framework for combating and preventing terrorism.[147]

Respect for human rights while countering terrorism has also been emphasized in international anti-terrorism conventions as well. For example, Article 12 of the International Convention for the Suppression of Acts of Nuclear Terrorism provides:

> Any person who is taken into custody or regarding whom any other measures are taken or proceedings are carried out pursuant to this Convention shall be guaranteed fair treatment, including enjoyment of all rights and guarantees in conformity with the law of the State in the territory of which that person is present and applicable provisions of international law, including the international law of human rights.

4.1.2   Regional Bodies, Human Rights and Counter-Terrorism

Respecting human rights and the rule of law principle are emphasized by the Council of Europe as follows: "Recalling that it is not only possible, but also absolutely necessary, to fight terrorism while respecting human rights, the rule of law and, where applicable, IHL." [148] Moreover, Article (II) of the Council of Europe Guidelines on

---

[146] United Nations, Peace and Security Section of the Department of Public Information, 'United Nations Counter-Terrorism Strategy Background Notes', 2009, p1 http://www.un.org/terrorism/pdfs/CT_Back ground_March_2009_terrorism2.pdf [1 March 2013].

[147] Organization for Security and Co-operation in Europe (OSCE), *Countering Terrorism, Protecting Human Rights: A Manual*, p 39.

[148] Council of Europe Guidelines on human rights and the fight against terrorism, Preamble (d).

human rights and the fight against terrorism provides: "All measures taken by States to fight terrorism must respect human rights and the principle of the rule of law, while excluding any form of arbitrariness, as well as any discriminatory or racist treatment."[149] Furthermore, the Guideline consists of provisions on the lawfulness of any anti-terrorist measures. Article (III) provides: "All measures taken by States to combat terrorism must be lawful."

Other regional conventions contain similar provisions. For instance, Article 15 of the Inter-American Convention against Terrorism provides: "The measures carried out by the States parties under this Convention shall take place with full respect for the rule of law, human rights, and fundamental freedoms."

The Organization for Security and Co-operation in Europe (OSCE) prepared a comprehensive framework for combating terrorism in the Bucharest Plan for Combating Terrorism, which recognizes terrorism as a threat to international peace and security. Furthermore, on the Plan of Action mandates that: "Early warning of and appropriate responses to violence, intolerance, extremism and discrimination against these groups and, at the same time, promote their respect for the rule of law, democratic values and individual freedoms."[150]

The Council of Europe Member States enacted three regional anti-terrorism conventions:

i.   The European Convention on the Suppression of Terrorism (1977) and Protocol thereto (2003).

ii.   The European Convention on the Prevention of Terrorism (2005).

iii. Conventions relating to cyber-crime and money laundering issues (2009).

Additionally, 17 guidelines on human rights and the fight against terrorism were issued by the Committee of Ministers of the Council of Europe on 2002 emphasizing State obligations to protect human rights. Each guideline, which places

---

[149] Council of Europe Guidelines on human rights and the fight against terrorism, II.
[150] Organization for Security and Co-operation in Europe (OSCE), The Bucharest Plan of Action for Combating Terrorism, 14 December 2001, paragraph 11 http://www.UNCHR.org/refworld/docid/47fdfb250.html [1 March 2013].

each right in the counter-terrorism context, is supported by law, case law and principles from international human rights institutions, in particular the European Court of Human Rights (ECtHR).[151]

Regional organizations have established human rights courts in the Americas, Europe, and Africa.[152] These courts review human rights cases and have the authority to overturn the domestic courts of the States that have accepted their contentious jurisdiction. Together, these courts have established a body of case law and legal opinions that have exponentially enriched the recognized jurisprudence of IHRL.[153]

4.1.3 Counter-Terrorism Measures as a Challenge for Human Rights

The relation between terrorism and human rights is extremely intensive. As the Special Rapporteur for the UN Sub-Commission on the Promotion and Protection of Human Rights, Kalliopi K. Koufa states, the pervasive impact of terrorism on human rights can be seen both directly and indirectly. Terrorist acts include, but are not limited to, murder, kidnapping, and seriously injuring innocent parties, which all deny victims their human rights to life, liberty, and dignity. The actions of terrorists not only deprive individuals of their rights to life, liberty, dignity, and democracy, but also foster an atmosphere of fear and dread that devastate social peace and public order.[154]

The indirect impact of terrorism has been rooted in the failure to abide number of fundamental rights of individuals by governments under the guise of counter-terrorism measures. Terrorist acts forced States widespread using security measures and implementing grave breaches of human rights. For instance, based on the Human Rights Watch World Report 2003 of the US:

---

[151] Organization for Security and Co-operation in Europe (OSCE), *Countering Terrorism, Protecting Human Rights: A Manual*, p 40.

[152] See, European Court of Human Rights; African Commission on Human and People's Rights; and Inter-American Court of Human Rights.

[153] Mark D. Kielsgard, 'A Human Rights Approach to Counter-Terrorism', p 278.

[154] Kalliopi K. Koufa. 07 June 1999. Preliminary Report 18, 'Terrorism and Human Rights'. *United Nations Economic and Social Council, , Sub-Commission on Prevention of Discrimination and Protection. of Minorities*. UN. Doc. EICN.4/Sub.2/1999/27.

Government policies adopted after the terrorist attacks of September 11 was marked by significant steps backward on human rights. The arbitrary detention of non-citizens, secret deportation hearings for persons suspected of connections to terrorism, the authorization of military commissions to try non-citizen terrorists, the failure to abide by the Geneva Conventions in the treatment of detainees held by the United States in Cuba, and the military detention without charge or access to counsel of U.S. citizens designated as "enemy combatants," were among the US actions that indicated the failure of the Bush administration to respect human rights. [155]

a) Human Rights and Terrorism: Bilateral Effects

The relationship between terrorism and human rights goes further than merely States counter-terrorism measures. A broader ramification exists beyond national security in the relationship between terrorism and human rights law. Some international human rights obligations may apply directly to non-State actors and some may apply indirectly to non-State actors.[156]

Counter-terrorism can impact human rights in a number of ways and at all stages of combating terrorism, including criminalizing terrorism in a wide and broad manner that leads to the criminalization of legitimate activities, such as lawful protests and expressions of opinion; prosecutions involving the violation of the right to fair trail; detentions that deny the right to *habeas corpus* or equivalent judicial procedure of suspected terrorist detainees before and during the detention period; and the lack of any clear legislative framework or counter-terrorism activities to detect, disrupt and prevent terrorist attacks.[157] Human rights also impacts counter-terrorism measures by providing a legal framework for counter-terrorism measures that requires States to struggle against terrorism while respecting human rights.

Terrorism and counter-terrorism both affect human rights, but some human rights challenged more that other rights in the context of counter-terrorism. Mary Robinson, UN High Commissioner for Human Rights; Walter Schwimmer, Secretary General of the Council of Europe; and Ambassador Gérard Stoudmann, Director of

---

[155] Human Rights Watch, 'World Report 2003: United States' http://www.hrw.org/wr2k3/us.htmi [11 April 2013].

[156] H. J. Steiner et al, *International Human Rights in Context*, p 384.

[157] United Nations Office of Drugs and Crime (UNODC), 'Frequently Asked Questions on International Law Aspects of Counter-Terrorism', pp 95-96.

the OSCE Office for Democratic Institutions and Human Rights, in a joint statement on 29 November 2001,[158] emphasized that:

> While we recognize that the threat of terrorism may require specific measures, we call on all governments to refrain from any excessive steps, which would violate fundamental freedoms and undermine legitimate dissent. Such steps might particularly affect the presumption of innocence, the right to a fair trial, freedom from torture, privacy rights, freedom of expression and assembly, and the right to seek asylum.

After the events of September 11, 2001, the international community has insisted that the response to terrorism must comply with basic standards of human rights and international law. For instance, SC Resolution 1456 (2003) insisted that any measures taken to combat terrorism must comply with international law, in particular with IHRL, refugee law and IHL.[159]

The following discussions will focus on the challenges of human rights after the September 11 attacks in the US.

4.1.4   Counter-Terrorism Measures: Human Rights Challenges Following September 11

The September 11 attacks in the US propelled the counter-terrorism phenomenon. SC Resolution 1373 obliged States to take all measures in the prevention of terrorist acts and bringing terrorists and their supporters to justice. The establishment of the CTC to monitor implementation of the Resolution's provisions is another reason for the global focus on counter-terrorism. While advocating the importance of combating terrorism on a global scale, international organizations expressed their concerns about the risk of human rights violations in light of some of the drastic counter-terrorism measures taken by States. For instance, the UN High Commissioner for Human Rights and UN Secretary General expressed the need to respect human rights while applying counter-terrorism measures undertaken by States.

---

[158] Joint statement issued by Mary Robinson, the UN High Commissioner for Human Rights, Walter Schwimmer, Secretary General of the Council of Europe, and Ambassador Gérard Stoudmann, Director of the OSCE's Office for Democratic Institutions and Human Rights http://www.unhchr.ch/h uricane/huricane.nsf/view01/4E59333FFC5341A7C 1256B13004C58F5 [12 November 2012].

[159] P. Hoffman, 'Human Rights and Terrorism' (2004) 26 *Human Rights Quarterly*, pp 941-942.

Following the increase of the terrorist attacks, especially after September 11, the international community enacted several treaties against terrorism in an ambit to reduce the risk of terrorism. The adoption of various international and regional instruments creates the assumption that the increase of international and regional anti-terrorism instruments may lead to debilitation of IHRL within the international community.

a) United States War on Terrorism: A challenge for Human Rights

Following the September 11 attacks in the US, the US waged a "war against terrorism". Although some governments supported the actions of the US, in reality the "war against terrorism" was waging a war against human rights and the international human rights framework. Furthermore, the legal concept of "war against terrorism" was questionable. The post-September 11 campaign to fight against terrorism led to the abuse of human rights, specifically the rights to liberty and security; the right to a fair trial; and the right to life.

Regarding the concept of the war, Hoffman asked if the "war on terrorism" is a "war", what sort of war it is? He added that, to date one of the characteristic of the "war on terrorism" is a refusal to accept that anybody of law applies of the way this war is waged. The picture painted by the US government is the "war on terrorism" is free from the constraints of international law. [160]

Cassese illustrates that the use of the term "war" by Bush Administration is inappropriate and is not paced under the subjects of international law. War is an armed conflict between two or more States, but the war against terrorism resulted from a serious terrorist attack by a non-State organization against a State. The use of the term 'war' has a grave psychological impact on public opinion and is intended to emphasize that the attack is so serious that it can be considered as aggression to the State and has to be responsive by all recourses as if in a state of war. [161]

---

[160] P. Hoffman, 'Human Rights and Terrorism', pp 939.
[161] A. Cassese, 'Terrorism is also Disrupting Some Crucial Legal Categories of International Law', p 993.

The call from the US for a global campaign against terrorism provides the context for several initiatives to tighten security legislation and to curb civil liberties. The "war against terrorism" will produce a significant shift in States' obligations to respect human rights. However, this battle against terrorism is understood as a fight for human rights. Here, the States are required to strike a balance between protecting the human rights of its citizens and other potential victims of terrorism; and protecting the human rights of alleged terrorists. [162]

b) Critiques on the United States Declaration of War against Terrorism

Fitzpatrick emphasizes neither war nor terrorism has a fixed meaning in contemporary international law. The post-September 11 events and the "war against terrorism" are characterized as follows:

i.   Undeclared international armed conflict by the US and its allies against Afghanistan and former Taliban regime;

ii.   An undeclared international armed conflict by US against the non-State entity Al-Qaeda;

iii. An internal armed conflict in Afghanistan between Taliban regime and its domestic rivals;

iv.   An undeclared international armed conflict by the US and its allies against a range of non-State entities and individuals alleged international terrorists.

v.   A continuation crime control activities against international terrorists, with a metaphorical use of "war" rhetoric.[163]

Vagts believes the US war against Taliban in Afghanistan could not be considered "war" under international law, arguing if there was a war between the US and Al-Qaeda/Taliban, it ceased when the US and its allies entered Kabul and the new government was recognized.[164]

---

[162] S. von Schorlemer, 'Human Rights: Substantive and Institutional Implications of the War against Terrorism', p 266.

[163] J. Fitzpatrick, 'Speaking Law to Power: The War against Terrorism and Human Rights', p 249.

[164] D. F. Vagts, 'Which Court Should Try Persons Accused of Terrorism', p 320.

The US Court of Appeals, in *Hamdi v Rumsfeld,* raised some issues that challenge the legality of the US "war on terrorism" as following:

> The court also questioned the government's most basic contentions regarding the ongoing hostilities, asking with whom is the war I should suggest that we're fighting? and will the war never be over as long as there is any member [or] any person who might feel that they want to attack the United States of America or the citizens of the United States of America?[165]

Donnelly and Mellon argue that the US response to suicide airplane bombing in New York and Washington has had predictably negative human rights consequences. Human rights have been restricted, infringed, violated, and ignored in many countries. Repression has been emboldened by this new global context. Alongside the negative points, some positive human rights consequences have arisen as well. Afghanistan has been freed from Taliban rule; the ongoing process of conflict resolution in Sri Lanka has been strengthened; and Pakistani supports from Kashmiri terrorists have been constrained.[166]

The refusal to accept that the rule of law governs the conduct of the "war on terrorism" has created an uncertainty and has also led to the erosion of individual rights.[167] For example, in response to queries and criticisms of the UN Special Rapporteur on Extrajudicial Arbitrary Executions in Yemen on November 2002, US delegates stated:

> The Government of the United States respectfully submits that inquiries related to allegations stemming from any military operations conducted during the course of an armed conflict with Al-Qaeda do not fall within the mandate of the Special Rapporteur.[168]

---

[165] *Yaser Esam Hamdi v. Donald Rumsfeld* [2002] No 02-7338 (United States District Court for the Eastern District of Virginia at Norfolk 8 January 2003), p 19 http://www.ca4.uscourts.gov/Opinions/Published/027338.P.pdf [22 February 2013].

[166] J. Donnelly et al, 'Human Rights and the War on Terror', (2005), *Human Rights and Human Welfare Review Digest,* p1 http://www.du.edu/korbel/hrhw/ researchdigest terror/in dex.html [17 October 2012].

[167] P. Hoffman, 'Human rights and Terrorism' (2004) 26 *Human Rights Quarterly,* pp 939-940.

[168] Letter dated 14 April 2003 from the Chief of Section, Political and Specialized Agencies, of the Permanent Mission of the United States of America to the United Nations Office at Geneva addressed to the secretariat of the Commission on Human Rights, UN Doc. E/CN.4/2003/G/80, (22 April 2003), p 2 http://www.unhchr.ch/Huridocda/Huridoca.nsf/0/9b67b6687466cfcac1256d2600514 c7f/$FILE/G0313804.pdf [22 February 2013].

The US challenge to the institutional competence or jurisdiction of the UN Human Rights Council,[169] was based on the contention that human rights law does not apply during armed conflicts.[170]

Conversely, Bates opines IHRL regulates States policies in counter-terrorism, in both peace and war. IHRL binds the States to respect and ensure general and specific civil and political rights; and requires States to act with due diligence to prevent violation of the right to life by non-State actors and regulates counter-terrorism law, policy, and practice. International human rights norms obligate States to criminalize investigate and prosecute certain terrorist acts based on specific terrorism conventions while attempting to protect individuals from torture, arbitrary detention, enforced disappearances and extrajudicial executions, which are often committed in the name of counter-terrorism.[171]

Regarding the applicability of the IHRL in wartime and outside of the national territory, the ICJ held in *Democratic Republic of Congo v Uganda* that:

> The Court first recalls that it had occasion to address the issues of the relationship between international humanitarian law and international human rights law and of the applicability of international human rights law instruments outside national territory.... It thus concluded that both branches of international law, namely international human rights law and international humanitarian law, would have to be taken into consideration.[172]

Furthermore, the ICJ, in the Advisory opinion of the Legal Consequences of the Construction of a Wall in the Occupied Palestinian Territory, opined that:

> The protection offered by human rights conventions does not cease in case of armed conflict, save through the effect of provisions for derogation of the kind to be found in Article 4 of the International Covenant on Civil and Political

---

[169] Letter dated 14 April 2003 from the Chief of Section, Political and Specialized Agencies, of the Permanent Mission of the United States of America to the United Nations Office at Geneva addressed to the secretariat of the Commission on Human Rights http://ap.ohchr.org/documents/alldocs.aspx?doc_id=3500 [22 February 2013].

[170] P. Alston et al, 'The Competence of the UN Human Rights Council and its Special Procedures in relation to Armed Conflicts: Extrajudicial Executions in the War on Terror' (2008) 19 (1) *The European Journal of International Law (EJIL)*, pp 185-186.

[171] E. Stubbins Batesand et al, *Terrorism and International Law, Accountability, Remedies, and Reforms*, 2011, Oxford University Press, New York, pp 77-79.

[172] International Court of Justice (ICJ) Report, 19 December 2005, p 243, paragraph 216 http://www.icj-cij.org/docket/index.php?p1=3&p2=5 [23 December 2012].

Rights. As regards the relationship between international humanitarian law and human rights law, there are thus three possible situations: some rights may be exclusively matters of international humanitarian law; others may be exclusively matters of human rights law; yet others may be matters of both these branches of international law.[173]

There is an indirect link between terrorism and the enjoyment of human rights. A State's response to terrorism may lead to the adoption of policies and practices that exceed the bounds of what is permissible under international law and the result in human rights violations. Counter-terrorism may affect human rights, particularly the right to fair trial; the presumption of innocence; privacy rights; and freedom from torture. However, if the "war on terrorism" is to be effective, it will have to include various restrictions against certain rights and freedoms. As a rule, all counter-terrorism measures must be in strict conformity with international law and IHRL.[174]

The following sections will discuss on some specific rights that violates more than other human rights by State's counter-terrorism measures. The specific rights examined include the right to life; the right to freedom from torture and cruel, inhuman or degrading treatment or punishment; the right to fair trial; and the right to privacy.

---

[173] International Court of Justice (ICJ) Report, 9 July 2004, p 178, paragraph 106 http://www.icj-cij.org/docket/index.php?p1=3&p2=5 [23 December 2012].
[174] S. von Schorlemer, 'Human Rights: Substantive and Institutional Implications of the War against Terrorism', pp 274- 275.

CHAPTER V

COUNTER-TERRORISM MEASURES: SPECIFIC HUMAN RIGHTS AT RISK OF VIOLATION

5.1   INTRODUCTION

In practice, adoption of strict counter-terrorism measures by some States has imposed serious dilemmas in relation to human rights. Employing repressive measures, such as the use of torture, against suspected terrorists undermines human rights and has led human rights advocates and activists to criticize such measures because of the corrosive effects on human rights. In the domestic dimension, some governments rushed to enact restrictive laws to prevent terrorism. However, these anti-terrorism laws undermine human rights.

The promotion and protection of human rights should be considered as the legal framework for the counter-terrorism measures. From the law enforcement perspective of counter-terrorism measures contains of policy and intelligence measure, all counter measures should be undertaken according to the respect for human rights and the rule of law.

Chapter V focuses on the violation of fundamental human rights while counter-terrorism and illustrates how human rights are at the risk of violation. To this aim numbers of case laws regarding the violation of specific human rights were analyzed. During the debates this chapter shows that despite the legality of some restrictions on human rights in special circumstances, these rights have to be respected and protect against any abuse by the States.

The State's counter-terrorism can negatively impact on the human rights norms. Among the human rights some rights are more at the risk of violation. For instance a number of instrumental human rights can be violated under the pretext of countering measures. The following paragraphs will discuss on specific rights, which are more at the subject of risk of abuse.

5.1.1   The Right to Life

Within international and regional legal instruments, the right to life is located at the summit of the hierarchy of rights in all human rights conventions.[175] This supreme right of a human being is enshrined within the UDHR as an absolute right even though is a non-binding international instrument, stating that "Everyone has the right to life, liberty and security of person." [176]

a) The Right to Life within International Instruments

The right to life is a non-derogable right and, according to regional and international instruments, States cannot invoke a war or public emergency to justify the arbitrary deprivation of life in counter-terrorism.[177] For example, Article 15(2) of the ECHR provides: "No derogation from Article 2, except in respect of deaths resulting from lawful acts of war, or from Articles 3, 4 (paragraph 1) and 7 shall be made under this provision."

The ICCPR in Article 4(2) prohibits any derogation from the inherent right to life that has been emphasized in Article 6.[178] In addition, the ACHR consists of provisions on prohibition of the arbitrary deprivation of life, providing that: "Every person has the right to have his life respected. This right shall be protected by law and, in general, from the moment of conception. No one shall be arbitrarily deprived of his life." [179]

---

[175] C. Tomuschat, 'Human Rights and International Humanitarian Law' (2010) 21 (1) *The European Journal of International Law (EJIL)*, p 16.

[176] Universal Declaration of Human Rights (UDHR), Art 3.

[177] International Covenant on Civil and Political Rights (ICCPR), Art 4(2): "2. No derogation from articles 6, 7, 8 (paragraphs I and 2), 11, 15, 16 and 18 may be made under this provision." See, American Convention on Human Rights (ACHR), Art 27(2), 3(17), (3)21.

[178] ICCPR, Art 4(2); European Convention on Human Rights (ECHR), Art 15(2), ACHR, Arts 27(2), 3(17), (3)21.

[179] ACHR, Art 4.

The Human Rights Committee, in General Comment 6, considered the protection against arbitrary deprivation of life as a supreme right from which no derogation is permitted, even in the time of public emergency. The Human Rights Committee stated that:

> The right to life enunciated in article 6 of the Covenant has been dealt with in all State reports. It is the supreme right from which no derogation is permitted even in time of public emergency which threatens the life of the nation. [180]

The ECHR protects this right in Article 2 and provides that deprivation of life is not a violation of the ECHR when the result from the use of force is no more than absolutely necessary. It reads as:

> Everyone's right to life shall be protected by law. No one shall be deprived of his life intentionally save in the execution of a sentence of a court following his conviction of a crime for which this penalty is provided by law. 2. Deprivation of life shall not be regarded as inflicted in contravention of this Article when it results from the use of force which is no more than absolutely necessary: (a) in defence of any person from unlawful violence; (b) in order to effect a lawful arrest or to prevent the escape of a person lawfully detained; (c) in action lawfully taken for the purpose of quelling a riot or insurrection.

Yet, as an exception, Article 15(2) ECHR allows lawful derogation in respect of death resulting from lawful acts of war, providing: "No derogation from Article 2, except in respect of deaths resulting from lawful acts of war ..."

b) The Right to Life at Risk of Violation

The following parts will discuss the two important challenges against the right to life by contemporary counter-terrorism measures.

I. Use of Lethal Force

The goal of the human rights framework is to strictly control not only of force intended to kill, but also of any unintended outcome involving deprivation of life. The use of lethal force by State agents in counter-terrorism is limited to the necessary situations. The condition of necessity has been approved by a number of international

---

[180] United Nations, Human Rights Committee, General Comment No 6 (1982) The Right to Life, (art. 6): 04/30/1982.CCPR , paragraph 1   http://www.unhchr.ch/tbs/doc.nsf/0/84ab9690ccd81fc 7c12563ed0046fae3 [17 December 2012].

human rights instruments and documents including Article 19 of the ICCPR, paragraph 294 the Inter-American Commission on Human Rights in its Report on Terrorism and Human Rights; paragraph 54 the Siracusa Principles on the Limitation and Derogation Provisions in the ICCPR; and the Code of Conduct for Law Enforcement Officials GA Resolution 34/169, 1979. Despite the non-binding nature of the Code of Conduct for Law Enforcement Officials, it specifically emphasizes two important conditions of use of force: necessity and "to the extent required for the performance of their duty."[181]

In its commentary on the necessary of the use of force by law enforcement officials, the Code of Conduct for Law Enforcement Officials provides:

> The use of force by law enforcement officials should be exceptional; while it implies that law enforcement officials may be authorized to use force as is reasonably necessary under the circumstances for the prevention of crime or in effecting or assisting in the lawful arrest of offenders or suspected offenders, no force going beyond that may be used.[182]

Moreover, the commentary further emphasizes the condition of proportionality of the use of force by the law enforcement officials, providing:

> National law ordinarily restricts the use of force by law enforcement officials in accordance with a principle of proportionality. It is to be understood that such national principles of proportionality are to be respected in the interpretation of this provision. In no case should this provision be interpreted to authorize the use of force which is disproportionate to the legitimate objective to be achieved.[183]

i.   Tennessee v Garner

The use of force applies to the seizing of individuals as well. A different context of the use of lethal force was applied by the US Supreme Court stated in the case of *Tennessee v Garner*, No 83-1035 in 1985. In October 1974 two Memphis Police Department Officers were summoned to stop a suspected burglary. As the police

---

[181] United Nations. 1979. *Code of Conduct for Law Enforcement Officials*, General Assembly Resolution 34/169, New York: United Nations http://www.unrol.org/files/CODEOF~1.PDF [23 February 2013].
[182] Code of Conduct for Law Enforcement Officials, Commentary (a), Art 3 http://www.ohchr.org/EN/ProfessionalInterest/Pages/LawEnforcementOfficials.aspx [23 February 2013].
[183] Code of Conduct for Law Enforcement Officials, Commentary (b), Article 3.

arrived, victim was seen fleeing the scene of the alleged burglary. An officer saw victim, and could see that victim possessed no weapon, and yelled at him to stop. The victim continued to climb the wall to escape at which point he was shot and killed. victim's father brought this action seeking damages for a violation of the Victim's constitutional rights. The judge found the officer's actions were constitutional. The Appellate Court reversed and the State appealed.[184] The US Supreme Court mentioned that: "The intrusiveness of a seizure by means of deadly force is unmatched. The use of deadly force also frustrates the interest of the individual, and of society, in judicial determination of guilt and punishment." [185] The Supreme Court's decision indicates that the use of deadly force against a nonviolent felon is not lawful.

Watkin believes the ability to seize an individual and to bring that person to justice requires two important factors:

i.   A law enforcement focus with a high level of physical control over the situation.

ii. Well-developed judicial process to deal with the offender.

He adds that the requisite factors are not met in terrorist involvements.[186]

ii.   United Nations Basic Principles on the Use of Force and Firearms by Law Enforcement Officials

The UN's Basic Principles on the Use of Force and Firearms by Law Enforcement Officials emphasizes the adoption of rules and regulations on the use of force and firearms,[187] stating:

> Governments and law enforcement agencies should develop a range of means as broad as possible and equip law enforcement officials with various types of weapons and ammunition that would allow for a differentiated use of force

---

[184]   Bloomberg   Law,   Case   briefs   of   Tennessee   v.   Garner http://www.casebriefs.com/blog/law/criminal-law/criminal-law-keyed-to-lafave/justification-and-excuse/tennessee-v-garner-4/] [22 February 2013].

[185] *Tennessee v. Garner* [1985] No. 83-1035 (United States Supreme Court 27 March 1985), p 471 http://supreme.justia.com/cases/federa l/us/471/1/ case.html [22 February 2013].

[186] K. Watkin, 'Controlling the Use of Force: A Role for Human Rights Norms in Contemporary Armed Conflict', pp 17-18

[187] K. Watkin, 'Controlling the Use of Force: A Role for Human Rights Norms in Contemporary Armed Conflict', p 18.

and firearms. These should include the development of non-lethal incapacitating weapons for use in appropriate situations, with a view to increasingly restraining the application of means capable of causing death or injury to persons. ... Law enforcement officials shall not use firearms against persons except in self-defence or defence of others against the imminent threat of death or serious injury...Ensure that firearms are used only in appropriate circumstances and in a manner likely to decrease the risk of unnecessary harm.[188]

The Basic Principle on the proportionality of the use of force further provides: "Whenever the lawful use of force and firearms is unavoidable, law enforcement officials shall: (a) Exercise restraint in such use and act in proportion to the seriousness of the offence and the legitimate objective to be achieved."[189]

iii. Neira Alegria v Peru

The IACtHR, in the judgment concerning the *Neira Alegria v Peru* case No 21 in 1996, placed emphasis on the limitations of the power of States to guarantee security and repeated its opinions from the cases of *Velasquez Rodriguez*[190] and *Godinez Cruz*.[191] On June 18, 1986, Victor Neira Alegria, Edgar Zenteno Escobar and William Zenteno Escobar were being detained at the correctional facility of San Juan Bautista, charged with the crime of terrorism. As a consequence of a riot at that correctional facility on the date indicated, the government delegated the control of the prisons to the Joint Command of the Armed Forces and that, as a result of this decision, the San Juan Bautista correctional facility was included in the so-called "Restricted Military Zones." The Inter-American Commission of Human Rights bring the case to IACtHR and further claims that those persons have been missing since the date on which the Armed Forces put down the riots and that their relatives have not seen or heard of them since. The IACtHR in 1996 held:

---

[188] Basic Principles on the Use of Force and Firearms by Law Enforcement Officials, Adopted by the Eighth United Nations Congress on the Prevention of Crime and the Treatment of Offenders, Havana, Cuba, 27 August to 7 September 1990, paragraphs 2, 10 (b) http://www2.ohchr.org/english/law/firearms.htm [22 February 2013].

[189] Basic Principles on the Use of Force and Firearms by Law Enforcement Officials, Adopted by the Eighth United Nations Congress on the Prevention of Crime and the Treatment of Offenders, Paragraph 5.

[190] *Velasquez Rodriguez v Honduras* [1988] Ser. C, No. 4 (Inter American Court of Human Rights 29 July 1988), paragraph 154 http://www1.umn.edu/humanrts/iachr/b_11_12d.htm [02 February 2013].

[191] *Godínez Cruz v Honduras* [1989] Ser. C, No. 5 (Inter American Court of Human Rights 20 January 1989), paragraph 162 http://www1.umn.edu/humanrts/iachr/C/5-ing.html [22 February 2013].

The power of the State is not unlimited, nor may the State resort to any means to attain its ends. The State is subject to law and morality. Disrespect for human dignity cannot serve as the basis for any State action.[192]

iv.   McKerr v United Kingdom

Once the use of force involves the killing of individuals, the right to life is violated. The case of *the McKerr v United Kingdom* No. 28883/95, 2001 in the ECtHR details the limits of the use of force in the case of killing and the importance of investigation to ensure the right to life of persons. On 11 November 1982, Jonathan McKerr was driving a car with two passengers when they were fired upon by police. All three victims were killed and the three officers were prosecuted for murder. On 5 June 1984, the judge held that there was insufficient evidence to establish guilt and acquitted the officers. Another application was made based on the violation against Article 2 of the European Convention of Human Rights (ECHR) in 1993 at the ECtHR. Article 2 of the ECHR provides:

> Everyone's right to life shall be protected by law. No one shall be deprived of his life intentionally save in the execution of a sentence of a court following his conviction of a crime for which this penalty is provided by law. 2. Deprivation of life shall not be regarded as inflicted in contravention of this article when it results from the use of force which is no more than absolutely necessary: a) in defence of any person from unlawful violence; b) in order to effect a lawful arrest or to prevent the escape of a person lawfully detained; c) in action lawfully taken for the purpose of quelling a riot or insurrection.

On 4 May 2001, the Court emphasized on the importance of the independent and effective investigations once a death be carried out and "unanimously finds a violation of Article 2 of the Convention." [193]

v.   McCann and Others v. United Kingdom

The issue of the limitation on use of force in the context of terrorism violence places emphasis on accountability processes, as is evident in the decision of the (ECtHR) in *McCann and Others v. United* Kingdom, No 18984/91 in 1995.[194] In 1988, the

---

[192] *Neira Alegria v Peru* [1995] Ser. C No. 21(Inter American Court of Human Rights 19 January 1995), paragraph 75 http://www.1.umn.edu/humanrts/iachr/C/20-ing.html [22 February 2013].

[193] *McKerr v. United Kingdom* [2001] No. 28883/95, (European Court of Human Rights, 4 May 2001), Human Rights Case Digest (2001) 12, pp 288-296.

[194] *McCann v. United Kingdom* [1995] 18984/91 (European Court of Human Rights 27 September 1995), http://hudoc.echr.coe.int/sites/eng/pages/search.aspx?i=001-57943 [23 February

Gibraltar police and British military personnel thwarted a planned IRA car bomb attack against a military unit's ceremonial parade at an assembly area. As the operation unfolded, however, all three suspects were shot multiple times by members of the Special Air Service and killed. The soldiers had feared that the terrorists were going to set off the bomb by means of a push-button remote device, but when the operation was over, no weapons or detonating devices were discovered. The ECtHR ruled that the soldiers' reflex action to shoot to kill lacks the degree of caution expected from law enforcement personnel in a democratic society.[195]

The Court's decision effectively guarantees the right to life while countering terrorism measures by placing emphasis on the proportionality, lawfulness, planning and control of activities involving anti-terrorism measures and operations. The Court articulated the limitations on the use of force as follows:

> Against this background, in determining whether the force used was compatible with Article 2 (art. 2), the Court must carefully scrutinize, as noted above, not only whether the force used by the soldiers was strictly proportionate to the aim of protecting persons against unlawful violence but also whether the anti-terrorist operation was planned and controlled by the authorities so as to minimize, to the greatest extent possible, recourse to lethal force.[196]

The nature of the threat and the circumstances within which force is applied will ultimately govern the choice of that framework. For example, when the violence used by terrorists reaches the level inflicted by Al-Qaeda on September 11, State action under human rights principles will find it less applicable than it was in McCann.[197]

vi.   Ergi v Turkey

2013]. See , Human Rights Case Digest, (1995) VI (5), pp 496-505.
[195] *McCann v. United Kingdom*, paragraph 212.
[196] *McCann v. United Kingdom*, paragraph 171.
[197] K. Watkin, 'Controlling the Use of Force: A Role for Human Rights Norms in Contemporary Armed Conflict', p 20.

In 1998, in the case of *Ergi v Turkey*, the ECtHR was ruled similarly. Ms. Havva Ergi lived in the village of Kesentas (South-East Turkey). On 29 September 1993, she was shot in the head while standing in a doorway leading onto the balcony of her house and killed instantly. The circumstances surrounding Ms. Ergi's death are a matter of dispute. The applicant claimed that the village was attacked indiscriminately by security forces, apparently in retaliation for the killing by members of the Workers' Party of Kurdistan (PKK) of a villager who had "collaborated" with the Government. The Government alleged that security forces had ambushed a PKK unit on the outskirts of the village, that Ms. Ergi was caught in the crossfire and that the bullet which killed her might well have been fired by a member of the PKK.[198]

The Court confirmed the violation of Article 2 of the ECHR on the right to life and mentioned that the State had failed to properly plan the counter-terrorism measures and operations. The Court stated:

> In keeping with the importance of this provision in a democratic society, the Court must, in making its assessment, subject deprivations of life to the most careful scrutiny, particularly where deliberate lethal force is used, taking into consideration not only the actions of the agents of the State who actually administer the force but also all the surrounding circumstances, including such matters as the planning and control of the actions under examination. [199]

vii.   Jean Charles de Mendez case

In another case of the killing of Jean Charles de Mendez in Stockwell Underground station by law enforcement officials thought were killing a suicide bomber by shot seven times in the head in July 2005, whereas the ECHR permits the use of lethal force only for a legitimate aim and absolutely necessary in Article 2 (2).[200] In 22 July 2005 during the course of a major Metropolitan Police anti-terrorist operation a number of undercover surveillance officers a number of armed firearms officers followed Jean Charles de Mendez onto the northbound Northern Line platform at Stockwell Underground station. Jean Charles had been under surveillance already

---

[198] *Ergi v. Turkey* [1998] No 40/1993/435/514,(European Court of Human Rights 28 July 1998) http://www.UNCHR.org/refworld/docid/3ae6b6291c.html [28 February 2013].
[199] *Ergi v. Turkey*, paragraph 79.
[200] I. Turner, 'Article 2 of the ECHR, the Investigative Obligation and the Shooting of Jean Charles de Mendezes' (2009) 5 *Web Journal of Current Legal Isuues*, p 1 http://webjcli.ncl.ac.uk/2009/issue5/pdf/turner5.pdf [28 February 2013].

when he left a block of flats. He stepped into the third coach of a stationary train and within moments two officers, aiming at his head, shot and killed him. It was their professed belief that he was a suicide bomber. Jean Charles had been followed in the erroneous belief that he was one Hussain Osman, a man suspected of having been responsible for a failed suicide bomb attack at the Shepherds Bush underground station the previous day. Jean Charles had nothing to do with terrorism and was, at the time of his death, travelling to work from his home address. He was unarmed; he was not carrying an explosive device.[201] The police officers were not prosecuted over the death of Jean Charles de Menezes based on the Court of London's decision as the primitive court. This case goes to High Court in 2006 and the case was closed when his family reaches a settlement with Scotland Yard.[202]

Generally, following a review of international and regional instruments, international documents, and legal cases, the use of force is not unlimited while countering terrorism by law enforcement officials in counter-terrorism measures. However, it has been limited based upon specific circumstances in light of proportionality and necessity.

The examination of treaties, case law and general principles of international law on the right to life established the following points:

i.   The right not to be arbitrary deprived of one's life is non-derogable.

ii. Positive measures to protect individuals within the jurisdiction must be taken by States in order to unlawful killing by the State agents, and must be investigated.

iii. Use of lethal force or firearms must be constructed narrowly and sharply limited.

iv. Counter-terrorism measures and operations which use force must be carefully planned and controlled to avoid the risk of violation against the right to life.[203]

---

[201] Independent Police Complaints Commission, Investigation into the shooting of Jean Charles de Menezes at Stockwell underground station on 22 July 2005 http://news.bbc.co.uk/2/shared/bsp/hi/pdfs/08_11_07_stockwell1.pdf [24 February 2013].

[202] D. Vikram, 'Jean Charles de Menezes' family settles for £100,000', Guardian London, 23 November 2009 http://www.guardian.co.uk/uk/2009/nov/23/jean-charles-de-menezes-settlement [24 February 2013].

[203] E. Stubbins Batesand et al, *Terrorism and International Law, Accountability, Remedies,*

II. Death Penalty

One century ago, capital punishment was routine everywhere. Nowadays, the big eight countries that retain the death penalty include China, India, Indonesia, Japan, Nigeria, Pakistan, Russia and the US. However, the execution still remains as a punishment within the criminal judicial system of some countries. [204]

i.   Death penalty within human rights instruments

Despite recognizing and emphasizing the "inherent right to life" of individuals by Article 6 (1) ICCPR, the Covenant recognizes the death penalty for the most serious crimes. Article 6 (2) provides:

> In countries which have not abolished the death penalty, sentence of death may be imposed only for the most serious crimes in accordance with the law in force at the time of the commission of the crime and not contrary to the provisions of the present Covenant and to the Convention on the Prevention and Punishment of the Crime of Genocide. This penalty can only be carried out pursuant to a final judgment rendered by a competent court.

In contrast, Optional Protocol 2 of the ICCPR obligates Member States to abolish the death penalty, stating: "Believing that abolition of the death penalty contributes to enhancement of human dignity and progressive development of human rights... Each State Party shall take all necessary measures to abolish the death penalty within its jurisdiction."[205]

The Office of High Commissioner of Human Rights, in paragraph seven of the General Comment No 6 on the right to life, opines that "The Committee is of the opinion that the expression "most serious crimes" must be read restrictively to mean that the death penalty should be a quite exceptional measure."

Furthermore, Article 1 Protocol No. 6 to the ECHR, Concerning the Abolition of the Death Penalty, provides: "The death penalty shall be abolished. No-one shall be

---

and Reforms, 2011, Oxford University Press, New York, p 93.

[204] S. C. Stafford, 'Killing the Death Penalty with Kindness', in David R. Dow at al, *Machinary of Death*, 2002, Routledge, New York, p 270.

[205] Second Optional Protocol to the International Covenant on Civil and Political Rights, Aiming at the Abolition of the Death Penalty (adopted by General Assembly Resolution 44/128 of 15 December 1989).

condemned to such penalty or executed."[206] Protocol No. 13 has repeated the exact provisions of Article 1 of the Protocol No. 6 within Article 1 of its text. However, Protocols No. 6 and 13 do not exclude the application of the death penalty in respect of acts committed in time of war or of imminent threat of war and the exception remains within both protocols. For instance, Protocol No. 6 of the ECHR provides:

> A State may make provision in its law for the death penalty in respect of acts committed in time of war or of imminent threat of war; such penalty shall be applied only in the instances laid down in the law and in accordance with its provisions.

Protocol No. 13 of the ECHR provides:

> Noting that Protocol No. 6 to the Convention, concerning the Abolition of the Death Penalty, signed at Strasbourg on 28 April 1983, does not exclude the death penalty in respect of acts committed in time of war or of imminent threat of war.[207]

The ICCPR emphasizes the prohibition of the use of the death penalty for pregnant women and children. Article 6 (5) clearly states: "Sentence of death shall not be imposed for crimes committed by persons below eighteen years of age and shall not be carried out on pregnant women." Furthermore, the provisions of the United Nations Convention on the Rights of the Child (UNCRC) contain of provisions concerning the prohibition of capital punishment for persons less than eighteen years of age. Article 37 (a) of the UNCRC reads: "No child shall be subjected to torture or other cruel, inhuman or degrading treatment or punishment. Neither capital punishment nor life imprisonment without possibility of release shall be imposed for offences committed by persons below eighteen years of age; ..."[208]

The Human Rights Committee frequently expresses its concerns regarding the existing use of capital punishment in the legal systems of some Member States. For

---

[206] Protocol No. 6 to the Convention for the Protection of Human Rights and Fundamental Freedoms Concerning the Abolition of the Death Penalty (adopted 28 April 1983, entered into force 1 November 1998) Art 1.

[207] Protocol No. 13 to the Convention for the Protection of Human Rights and Fundamental Freedoms Concerning the Abolition of the Death Penalty in All Circumstances (adopted 3 May 2002, entered into force 1 July 2003) Paragraph 4.

[208] United Nations Convention on the Rights of the Child (adopted 20 November 1989, entered into force 2 September 1990) UNTS (UNCRC), Art 37.

example, in its Concluding Observations 1995 about the existing use of capital punishment in Estonia, it was noted that:

> The Committee is concerned that the death penalty can still be imposed in Estonia for crimes which cannot be qualified as the most serious crimes under article 6 of the Covenant. Moreover, the Committee notes with concern that, despite the drafting of a new Criminal Code that will abolish capital punishment, recent amendments to the current Criminal Code have added two more crimes to the list of those punished by capital punishment.[209]

Nowadays, terrorist acts have reached such a degree of seriousness that the members of the international community realize how poorly drafted anti-terrorist strategies can be. Terrorism has assumed the future of a globalized criminal activity able to reach and hit any State and its residents.[210] These issues are placed terrorist crimes in a category of serious and organized crimes. In addition, international and regional anti-terrorism conventions and related documents have emphasized the seriousness of terrorist crimes. For example, Article 4(b) of the International Convention for the Suppression of the Financing of Terrorism stresses on the grave nature of terrorist offences as follows: "To make those offences punishable by appropriate penalties which take into account the grave nature of the offences."

Article 5 (b) International Convention for the Suppression of Acts of Nuclear Terrorism contains of similar provisions on the gravity and seriousness of terrorist crime. Therefore, the existence of a death sentence for persons involved in terrorist activities depends on the domestic legal system of the State.

ii.   Existence of death penalty within the United States military commissions

---

[209] United Nations, Human Rights Committee, Concluding Observations of the Human Rights Committee: Estonia, (9 November 1995) CCPR/C/79/Add.59, paragraph 17 http://www.UNCHR. org/refworld/docid/3ae6b02718.html [13 October 2012].

[210] M. D. Filippo, 'Terrorist Crimes and International Co-operation: Critical Remarks on the Definition and Inclusion of Terrorism in the Category of International Crimes' (2008) 19 (3) *The European Journal of International Law (EJIL)*, p 535.

The use of the death penalty by the US Military Commission that was established by Military Order November 13, 2001[211] undermines the human rights goal of the eventual abolition of the death penalty, especially in the light of the international community's efforts toward the abolition of the death penalty in the Rome Statute.[212] The MCA 2006 provides:

> A military commission under this chapter may, under such limitations as the Secretary of Defence may prescribe, adjudge any punishment not forbidden by this chapter, including the penalty of death when authorized under this chapter or the law of war.[213]

Some experts have criticized the potential use of the death penalty against Guantanamo Bay detainees that are accused of terrorist acts under the military commission's jurisdiction. For instance, Eric Freedman stated that the trials of the detainees will be a "historic challenge" for prosecutors and noted that a decision to seek the death penalty will draw intense scrutiny to the proceedings both legally and politically from around the world. Tom Fleener noted that seeking the death penalty could also bog down the military court system.[214]

MCA 2009 authorizes the death penalty in Section 948d as follows:

> A military commission under this chapter shall have jurisdiction to try persons subject to this chapter for any offense made punishable by this chapter, sections 904 and 906 of this title (articles 104 and 106 of the Uniform Code of Military Justice), or the law of war, whether such offense was committed before, on, or after September 11, 2001, and may, under such limitations as the President may prescribe, adjudge any punishment not forbidden by this chapter, including the penalty of death when specifically authorized under this chapter. A military commission is a competent tribunal to make a finding sufficient for jurisdiction.

Moreover, section 949 (m) (2) provides:

---

[211] Military Order Detention, Treatment, and Trial of Certain Non-Citizens in the War Against Terrorism, United States Presidential Document, 13 November 2001 https://www.fas.org/irp/off docs/eo/mo-111301.htm [22 October 2012].

[212] P. Hoffman, 'Human Rights and Terrorism', pp 941-942.

[213] Section 984d (d) Military Commission Act 2006.

[214] Death Penalty Information Centre (DPIC), 'U.S. to Seek Death Penalty under New Military Commissions' http://www.deathpenaltyinfo.org/us-seek-death-penalty-under-new-military-commiss ions [25 February 2013].

No person may be sentenced to death by a military commission, except insofar as (A) the penalty of death has been expressly authorized under this chapter, chapter 47 of this title, or the law of war for an offense of which the accused has been found guilty.

iii.   US v Khalid Sheikh Mohammed

The US v Khalid Sheikh Mohammed, et al is the trial of five alleged Al-Qaeda members for aiding the September 11 attacks. They were charged under the MCA 2006 with attacking civilians, attacking civilian objects, intentionally causing serious bodily injury, murder in violation of the law of war, destruction of property in violation of the law of war, hijacking or hazarding a vessel or aircraft, terrorism, and providing material support for terrorism.[215]

The trial began on 5 June 2008 in a military commission and transferred in July 2009 to the U.S. District Court for the Southern District of New York. For the security reasons, on 21 January 2010 all charges have been withdrawn in the military commissions being held at Guantanamo Bay. On 5 May 2012 the trail was started again in Guantanamo Bay.[216] The case is still open in military commission and if convicted, the five will face the death penalty despite of a number of NGOs critiques namely, Human Rights Watch, AI, CCR and the US military defence lawyer's.

III. Extrajudicial Executions (Targeted Killings)

The term "extrajudicial execution" has no explicit definition in treaty law or non-binding international legal standards. Amnesty International, in its 14-Point Program for the Prevention of Extrajudicial Executions, defines it as "unlawful or deliberate killing" carried out by order of a government or with its complicity or acquiescence.[217]

---

[215] *The US v. Khalid Sheikh Mohammed* [2008] (Military Commissions 15 April 2008) www.Findlaw.com [02 March 2013].

[216] 'Khalid Sheikh Mohammed Guantanamo hearing gets chaotic start', BBC News, 6 May 2012 http://www.bbc.co.uk/news/world-us-canada-17966362 [02 March 2013].

[217] E. Stubbins Batesand et al, *Terrorism and International Law, Accountability, Remedies, and Reforms*, p 95.

i. Extrajudicial executions and applicable law

Cassel believes that the main legal provision applicable to targeted killing is Article 6(1) ICCPR, which protects the inherent right to life. Yet, not all extrajudicial killings are arbitrary. In limited circumstances, such as conditions based on necessity and urgency, terrorist suspects may be executed if they are about the commit an imminent attack on life and there is no time to arrest them.[218]

Regarding targeted killings outside of the armed conflicts, Tomuschat analyzes the ICJ advisory opinion on nuclear arms in 1996[219] and argues that there is a lack of clarity regarding the connotation which the court attached to those words. On one hand, the court supports the doctrine of separation between the application of IHL and IHRL. On the other hand, the Court wanted to highlight that Article 6 of the ICCPR has to be understood in conjunction with rules of IHL.[220] The ICJ opined as follows:

> Whether a particular loss of life, through the use of a certain weapon in warfare, is to be considered an arbitrary deprivation of life contrary to Article 6 of the Covenant, can only be decided by reference to the law applicable in armed conflict and not deduced from the terms of the Covenant itself.[221]

On one hand, granting license to State authorities to kill suspected enemies is considered an abuse of State power. On the other hand, one cannot simply dismiss the parallel drawn by the States involved between the legitimate killing of enemy combatants during an armed conflict and the targeting of active members of terrorist organizations that have, for all intents and purposes, declared war against the attacked State.[222]

---

[218] D. Cassel, 'International Human Rights and the United States Response to 11 September', in C. Fijnaut et al, *Legal Instruments in the Fight against International Terrorism: A Transatlantic Dialogue*, 2004, Brill Academic Publishers, pp 268-269.

[219] International Court of Justice (ICJ), Advisory Opinion on the Legality of the Threat for Use of Nuclear Weapons (the Nuclear Weapon Case) (8 July 1996).

[220] C. Tomuschat, 'Human Rights and International Humanitarian Law', pp17-18.

[221] International Court of Justice (ICJ), Advisory Opinion on the Legality of the Threat for Use of Nuclear Weapons.

[222] D. Kretzmer, 'Targeted Killing of Suspected Terrorists: Extra-Judicial Executions or Legitimate Means of Defence?' (2005) 16 (2) *The European Journal of International Law (EJIL)*, p 174.

ii.   The United States Drone Attacks: The Special Rapporteur of the UN Commission of Human Rights (UNCHR) Report

On 3 November 2002, six suspected Al-Qaeda members, including an Al-Qaeda chief wanted in connection with the bombing of the USS Cole, were killed in Yemen when a CIA drone (unmanned aerial vehicle) launched a "Hellfire" missile and struck the car in which they were traveling. It was the first direct US strike against the Al-Qaeda network outside Afghanistan since the US led "war on terrorism" began after the September 11 terrorist attacks.[223] Following this attack, the Special Rapporteur of the United Nations Commission of Human Rights (UNCHR), Asma Jahangir, sent a communication to the US Government on 15 November 2002 querying whether the alleged attack was consistent with applicable international legal norms. In response, the US rejected the competence and mandate of the UNCHR and mentioned that the targeted killing did not fall within the competence of the Human Rights Council, in general, or that of the Special Rapporteur, in particular.[224]

The US responded to the Special Rapporteur of the UNCHR on exclusion of IHRL in armed conflict based on the following four propositions:

i.   The US is engaged in a war against terrorism, specifically with Al-Qaeda, in Afghanistan.

ii.   IHL is the only applicable law during an armed conflict and operates as the exclusion of human rights in the war situations.

iii.   The mandate of the Human Rights Council and its special procedures are limited to IHRL

iv.   The Human Rights Council and its special procedures lack competence to address within the framework of the US "war on terrorism"

iii.   The applicable law in the war on terrorism: The International Court of Justice (ICJ) position

These reasons are challenged by Alston and others in light of the Advisory Opinion of the ICJ in Nuclear Weapons, where the ICJ stated: "The test of what is an arbitrary

---

[223] 'US kills Cole suspect', CNN, 5 November 2002 http://www.cnn.com/2002/ WORLD/meast/11/04/yemen.blast/index.html [26 February 2013].

[224] P. Alston et al, 'The Competence of the UN Human Rights Council and its Special Procedures in relation to Armed Conflicts: Extrajudicial Executions in the War on Terror' (2008) 19 (1) *The European Journal of International Law (EJIL)*, pp 185-186.

deprivation of life, however, then falls to be determined by the applicable *lex specialis*,[225] namely, the law applicable in armed conflict which is designed to regulate the conduct of hostilities. ...".[226]

Therefore, the IHL and the IHRL are not complementary, but mutually exclusive. The US reasons challenged by reviewing the history of the UNCHR and now the Council that improved the competence of the Special Rapporteurs in the issues of IHL. For example in Resolution 1992/S-1/1 on human rights in the former Yugoslavia,[227] and Resolution S-3/1 on human rights in Rwanda,[228] the Commission called to ensure full respect for humanitarian law, and Resolution 1996/68 to the Government of Israel for occupying of territories in Southern Lebanon and West Bekaa to comply with Geneva Convention of 1994.[229] The US position is the Special Rapporteurs' mandates should cease to consider any allegations of violations received from victims of the conflicts and in all situations in which widespread and grave abuses of human rights have been reported.[230]

iv.   **The applicable law in the war on terrorism: The Parliamentary Assembly of the Council of Europe (PACE) position**

The PACE produced a report outlining the CIA intention to kill captured and detained high value terrorism suspects. To this aim, the US created two detention centres in Poland and Romania. The order to Kill-Capture Detain (KCD) suspected terrorists was authorized by the lawyers of the CIA and the Bush Administration.[231] The exact number and identities of people subject to KCD orders; the number and identities of

---

[225] Originally a Latin word that in English means "Special law".

[226] International Court of Justice (ICJ), Advisory Opinion on the Legality of the Threat for Use of Nuclear Weapons.

[227] United Nations Commission on Human. Rights, The situation of human rights in the territory of the former Yugoslavia, 1992, Resolution 1992/S-1/1, paragraph 1, http://www1.umn.edu/humanrts/commission/country52/9-yug.htm [26 February 2013].

[228] United Nations Commission on Human Rights, Human rights in Rwanda, 1994, Resolution S-3/1 http://www1.umn.edu/humanrts/commission/country51/12.htm [26 February 2013].

[229] United Nations Commission on Human Rights, Human rights situation in southern Lebanon and West Bekaa, 1996, Resolution 1996/68, http://unispal.un.org/UNISPAL.NSF/0/4B54E18E7F172B B885256CCD0055EFB9 [26 February 2013].

[230] P. Alston et al, 'The Competence of the UN Human Rights Council and its Special Procedures in relation to Armed Conflicts: Extrajudicial Executions in the War on Terror', pp 191-208.

[231] E. Stubbins Batesand et al, *Terrorism and International Law, Accountability, Remedies, and Reforms*, p 96.

persons rendered to third countries for interrogation; and the number and identities of individuals held in secret CIA "black sites" are still unconfirmed.[232]

Nowak argues that the US-led strategy of combating terrorism outside the rule of law and outside minimum standards of IHRL and IHL by resorting to systematic practices of arbitrary detention; enforced disappearance; torture; denial of *habeas corpus*; and minimum standards of a fair trial constitutes gross and systematic human rights violations and may even be considered crimes against humanity. The global spider web of secret detention facilities; torture chambers; and so-called extraordinary rendition flights operated by the CIA with private chartered aircraft for the purpose of circumventing the requirements of international aviation law can no longer be concealed.[233]

v.   **The applicable law in the war on terrorism: The International Committee of the Red Cross (ICRC) position**

Regarding the appropriate law to be applied in the "war on terrorism", the International Committee of the Red Cross (ICRC) stated the following in regards to the relevance of IHL in the context of terrorism:

> International humanitarian law (the law of armed conflict) recognizes two categories of armed conflict: international and non-international. When and where the "global war on terror" manifests itself in either of these forms of armed conflict, international humanitarian law applies, as do aspects of international human rights and domestic law. When armed violence is used outside the context of an armed conflict in the legal sense or when a person suspected of terrorist activities is not detained in connection with any armed conflict, humanitarian law does not apply. Instead, domestic laws, as well as international criminal law and human rights govern. Whether or not an international or non-international armed conflict is part of the "global war on terror" is not a legal, but a political question. The designation "global war on terror" does not extend the applicability of humanitarian law to all events included in this notion, but only to those which involve armed conflict.[234]

---

[232] M. Satterthwaite, 'The US Program of Extraordinary Rendition and Secret Detention: Past and Future', in *CIA Extraordinary Rendition Flights, Torture and. Accountability: A European Approach*, European Centre for Constitutional and Human rights (ECCHR), Germany, 2008, p 33 http://www.ecchr.de/index.php/ecchr-publications/articles/publications.html [28 February 2013].

[233] M. Nowak, *CIA Extraordinary Rendition Flights, Torture and. Accountability: A European Approach*, 2008, p 9.

[234] The International Committee of the Red Cross (ICRC) Resources Centre, 'The relevance of IHL in the context of terrorism' 2011 http://www.icrc.org/eng/resources/documents/misc/ terrorism-ihl-210705.htm [26February 2013].

In the context of the "war on terror", although counter-terrorism measures are employed in an armed conflict where IHL is applicable, this does not mean that IHRL should not be applied alongside IHL. However, where counter-terrorism measures are employed outside of armed conflicts, IHL does not apply. Therefore, in the fight against terrorism, in both the military and law enforcement counter-terrorism approaches, IHRL governs counter-terrorism measures irrespective of whether they are undertaken in the context of an armed conflict or not. However, the applicability of the IHL depends upon the existence of an armed conflict.

vi.   The applicable law and the rights of detained persons in armed conflicts: The United States position

The US argues that IHL is the appropriate law in situations of armed conflict and emphasizes the exclusion of IHRL during such times on the basis of the separation of the respective scopes of IHL and IHRL. The sentiment is illustrated within the following response of US delegates to the Special Rapporteur's letter:

> International humanitarian law is the applicable law in armed conflict and governs the use of force against legitimate military targets. Accordingly, the law to be applied in the context of an armed conflict to determine whether an individual was arbitrarily deprived of his or her life is the law and customs of war. Under that body of law, enemy combatants may be attacked unless they have surrendered or are otherwise rendered hors de combat. Al-Qaeda terrorists who continue to plot attacks against the United States may be lawful subjects of armed attack in appropriate circumstances.[235]

The ICRC, in international and non-international armed conflicts, confirms this view and states that:

> IHL rules governing international or non-international armed conflicts... In both situations, IHL must be observed by all parties and the rules on the conduct of hostilities, the treatment of the wounded, prisoners and civilians, apply to all. IHL does not apply when terrorist acts occur, or persons suspected of terrorism are detained, outside an armed conflict.[236]

---

[235] Letter dated 14 April 2003 from the Chief of Section, Political and Specialized Agencies, of the Permanent Mission of the United States of America to the United Nations Office at Geneva addressed to the secretariat of the Commission on Human Rights, UN Doc. E/CN.4/2003/G/80, (22 April 2003), p 4 http://www.unhchr.ch/Huridocda/Huridoca.nsf/0/9b67b6687466cfcac1256d2600514 c7f/$FILE/G0313804.pdf [22 February 2013].

[236] The International Committee of the Red Cross (ICRC), 'Challenges for IHL - terrorism: overview', 29 October 2010 http://www.icrc.org/eng/war-and-law/contemporary-challenges-for-ihl/terrorism/overview-terrorism.htm [26 February 2013].

vii.   The rights of detained persons in armed conflicts: The International Committee of the Red Cross (ICRC) position

Although the ICRC in expression of its mandates and duties in the condition of the rights of detained persons in the fight against terrorism exceeds its competences and separates the situations to the international and non-international armed conflicts as follows:

> If they are detained in an international armed conflict, the ICRC must be granted access to them under the relevant IHL rules. When the fight against terrorism involves a non-international armed conflict, the ICRC offers its humanitarian services to the parties. Outside armed conflict situations, the ICRC exercise its right of humanitarian initiative to request access to persons detained.

In the context of the US "war on terror" and the military approach towards counter-terrorism measures by the US in Afghanistan and Iraq, the ICRC clearly recognizes the US war in Afghanistan and Iraq as armed conflicts[237] and emphasizes the applicability of IHL and IHRL in both situations. Therefore, the appropriate laws from which to develop a legal framework for the wars consist of both IHL and IHRL because IHRL and IHL are complementary, not exclusive, legal regimes.

viii.   The rights of detained persons in armed conflicts: Working Group of Special Rapporteurs position

The US position concerning the targeted killing of suspected terrorists was challenged by the UNCHR report in February 2006. A Working Group of Special Rapporteurs on the situation of detainees captured by the US in the course of an armed conflict or outside of an armed conflict challenged the US position concerning the targeted killing through the global fight against terrorism following the September 11. The report states:

> Because detention "without charges or access to counsel for the duration of hostilities" amounts to a radical departure from established principles of human rights law, it is particularly important to distinguish between the detainees captured by the United States in the course of an armed conflict and those captured under circumstances that did not involve an armed conflict. In

---

[237] Official Statement of the International Committee of the Red Cross (ICRC), 'The relevance of IHL in the context of terrorism', 2005, in UN Commission on Human Rights, *Situation of Detainees at Guantanamo Bay*, 27 February 2006, No: E/CN.4/2006/120, p 29 http://www.UNCHR.org/refworld/country,,UNCHR,,CUB,,45377b0b0,0.html [26 February 2013].

this context, it is to be noted that the global struggle against international terrorism does not, as such, constitute an armed conflict for the purposes of the applicability of international humanitarian law. [238]

Apparently, the global fight against terrorism is not recognized as an armed conflict, which consequently eliminates the applicability of IHL. Arguably, the intent of the UNCHR Rapporteurs was not to limit the application of IHL in counter-terrorism measures within this part of their joint detailed report. In actuality, the Rapporteurs sought to expand the range of the UNCHR Rapporteurs authority to the majority of situations to maximize the protection of human rights, although it is not apparent in this portion of the joint report. In addition to considering the applicability of IHL and IHRL in the context of terrorism issues, each case should be reviewed on a case by case basis. For example this part of the Rapporteurs' report has to be observed in the case of detention without charge of detained persons in the hostilities and must not distribute to other situations and protective norms.

ix.   Kretzmer's three models of counter-terrorism in the issue of targeted killing
Kretzmer categorizes the issue of targeted killing into three models as follows:

i.   Law enforcement model.

ii.   Armed conflict model.

iii. Mixed model.

In the law enforcement model, the applicable law is IHRL and the use of lethal force can be justified in very limited conditions. While IHL is the applicable law in the armed conflict model, some debates rise on the international and non-international conflicts that the applicable law is the humanitarian law and the Geneva Conventions and Article 1 (1) of Additional Protocol II. In addition to the armed conflict with

---

[238] Leila Zerrougui; the Special Rapporteur on the independence of judges and lawyers, Leandro Despouy; the Special Rapporteur on torture and other cruel, inhuman or degrading treatment or punishment, Manfred Nowak; the Special Rapporteur on freedom of religion or belief, Asma Jahangir; and Paul Hunt the Special Rapporteur on the right of everyone to the enjoyment of the highest attainable standard of physical and mental health. 2006. E/CN.4/2006/120, Economic, Social and Cultural Rights Civil and Political Rights, *United Nations, Economic and Social Council, Commission on Human Rights*. Report on the situation of detainees at Guantanamo Bay. New York: United Nations. Paragraph 19 http://news.bbc.co.uk/2/shared/bsp/hi/pdfs/16_02_06_un_guantanamo .pdf [23 July 2013].

terrorist as international armed conflict, Kretzmer opines that Cassese regards suspected terrorists as civilians unless taking direct part in hostilities. Such a restricted theory makes the right of self-defence under Article 51 of the UN Charter meaningless. Kretzmer finds this theory unacceptable. In the case of armed conflict with terrorist as non-international armed conflict, the general assumption is that violence involving non-State actors is a matter of domestic law and the law enforcement model should be followed. The mixed model covers the problem of the law enforcement models; the applicability of IHRL in armed conflicts as alleged by the US; and the problem of an armed conflict between a State and a transnational terrorist group, which is arguably not an international conflict despite transcending borders. Hence, the only acceptable justification for targeting suspected terrorists is the protection of potential victims of terrorist attacks by the use of lethal force in situations deemed necessary in the subject of law enforcement jurisdiction and in the lack of law enforcement jurisdiction by the principle of necessity under Article 51 of the UN Charter.[239]

5.1.2   Right to Free from Torture and Cruel, Inhuman or Degrading Treatment or Punishment

The right to freedom from torture and cruel, inhuman or degrading treatment or punishment is an absolute right of individuals that is protected by various international and regional instruments. This right cannot be derogated even in times of emergency. This right within IHRL and IHL instruments will be discussed within the following paragraphs.

a)   Definition of Torture

The prohibition against torture is a peremptory norm of international law (*jus cogens*) and non-derogable,[240] even in the time of public emergency. The prohibition forms part of customary international law, which means that is binding on every member of

---

[239] D. Kretzmer, 'Targeted Killing of Suspected Terrorists: Extra-Judicial Executions or Legitimate Means of Defence?', pp 175-204.
[240] *Belgium v. Senegal* [2012] ICJ (International Court of Justice 20 July 2012), Questions relating to the Obligation to Prosecute or Extradite, No 2012/24, p 6.

international community regardless of whether the State has ratified conventions that condemn torture. Any practice of torture constitutes a crime against humanity.[241]

In 1986, the World Health Organization working group introduced the concept of organized violence, which was defined as:

> The inter-human infliction of significant, avoidable pain and suffering by an organized group according to a declared or implied strategy, and or system of ideas and attitudes. It comprises any violent action that is unacceptable by general human standards, and relates to the victims' feelings. Organized violence includes "torture, cruel inhuman or degrading treatment or punishment.[242]

Amnesty International presents a simple and clear definition of torture as: "The systematic and deliberate infliction of acute pain by one person on another, or on a third person, in order to accomplish the purpose of the former against the will of the latter."[243]

The Optional Protocol to the Convention against Torture 2006 (OPCAT) ensures the practical protection of detainees against torture and other cruel inhuman or degrading treatments through the recommendations of the subcommittee and the subcommittee performing visits to places. The establishment of a Subcommittee on Prevention of Torture and Other Cruel, Inhuman or Degrading Treatment or Punishment (SPT) was the product of a convention to observe and access to the places of detention of State Parties. Article 11 of the Protocol provides: "The Subcommittee on Prevention shall: (a) Visit the places referred to in article 4 and make recommendations to States Parties concerning the protection of persons deprived of their liberty against torture and other cruel, inhuman or degrading treatment or punishment."

---

[241] Office of the High Commissioner for Human Rights (OHCHR), 'Fact sheet 4' (2002) http://www.ohchr.org/Documents/Publications/FactSheet4rev.1en.pdf [12 October 2102].
[242] World Health Organization (WHO). 1986. Report from the programme on Health Service Research. The Health Hazards of Organized Violence. *WHO Meeting, Veldhoven.* Copenhagen: Regional Office for Europe http://www.ucl.ac.uk/clinical-psychology/Research-Groups/PainSIG/definitions.htm [12 October 2012].
[243] Amnesty International, 'Torture in the Eighties' (1973) http://www.ucl.ac.uk/clinical-psychology/Research-Groups/PainSIG/definitions.htm [12 October 2012].

b) Prohibition against Torture and Cruel, Inhuman or Degrading Treatment or Punishment within International Human Rights Law in Counter-terrorism Measures

States have a duty to prevent torture, but it is not often applied in practice. A lack of understanding exists about the concept of torture prevention. According to Chambers Dictionary, "to prevent" means "to stop". Any intervention in the fight against torture is described as prevention. Generally there are two types of torture prevention. The first type is direct prevention (mitigation) that happens before torture takes place, which aims to prevent torture from occurring by reducing the risk factors and eliminating the possible causes. The second type is indirect prevention (deterrence), which takes place after torture has occurred and focuses on avoiding the repetition of such acts through investigation, denunciation, litigation, prosecution and other actions.[244]

I. Prohibition of Torture within International Human Rights Instruments

The majority of international human rights instruments condemn torture in their provisions. For example, Article 5 of the UDHR provides: "No one shall be subjected to torture or to cruel, inhuman or degrading treatment or punishment." In addition, the prohibition against torture cruel, inhuman or degrading treatment or punishment is enshrined within Article 7 of the ICCPR; Article 3 of the ECHR; and Article 5(2) of the ACHR as well. For instance Article 7 ICCPR states: "No one shall be subjected to torture or to cruel, inhuman or degrading treatment or punishment. In particular, no one shall be subjected without his free consent to medical or scientific experimentation." Furthermore, Article 3 of the ECHR emphasizes on prohibition of torture and states: "No one shall be subjected to torture or to inhuman or degrading treatment or punishment."

A number of international and regional human rights conventions and documents prohibit torture and any cruel or inhumane treatment.[245] Specifically the

---

[244] Office of the High Commissioner for Human Rights (OHCHR), Association for Prevention of Torture (APT), and Asia Pacific Forum of National Human Rights Institutions (APF), 'Preventing Torture: An Operational Guide for National Human Rights Institutions' (2010), pp 9-10 http://www .ohchr.org/Documents/Countries/NHRI/Torture_Prevention_Guide.pdf [12 October 2012].
[245] See, Standard Minimum Rules for the Treatment of Prisoners (1955), Code of Conduct for Law Enforcement Officials (1979),Basic Principles on the Use of Force and Firearms by Law Enforcement Officials (1990), Principles of Medical Ethics relevant to the Role of Health Personnel,

UN adopted CAT on 10 December 1984.[246] The recent convention is the result of adoption of the Declaration on the Protection of all Persons from Being Subjected to Torture and other cruel, Inhuman or Degrading Treatment or Punishment (Torture Declaration).[247]

The Declaration on the Protection of All Persons from Being Subjected to Torture and Other Cruel, Inhuman or Degrading Treatment or Punishment, the predecessor of the CAT, defined torture within Article 1 as any intentional physical or mental act against person which causes pain or suffering as follows:

> Torture means any act by which severe pain or suffering, whether physical or mental, is intentionally inflicted by or at the instigation of a public official on a person for such purposes as obtaining from him or a third person information or a confession, punishing him for an act he has committed or is suspected of having committed, or intimidating him or other persons. It does not include pain or suffering arising only from, inherent in or incidental to, lawful sanctions to the extent consistent with the Standard Minimum Rules for the Treatment of Prisoners.

CAT within Article 1 defines torture in similar terms as follows:

> The term "torture" means any act by which severe pain or suffering, whether physical or mental, is intentionally inflicted on a person for such purposes as obtaining from him or a third person information or a confession, punishing him for an act he or a third person has committed or is suspected of having committed, or intimidating or coercing him or a third person, or for any reason based on discrimination of any kind, when such pain or suffering is inflicted by or at the instigation of or with the consent or acquiescence of a public official or other person acting in an official capacity. It does not include pain or suffering arising only from, inherent in or incidental to lawful sanctions.

---

particularly Physicians, in the Protection of Prisoners and Detainees against Torture and Other Cruel, Inhuman or Degrading Treatment or Punishment (1982), Body of Principles for the Protection of All Persons under Any Form of Detention or Imprisonment (1988), Basic Principles for the Treatment of Prisoners (1990), Rome Statute of the International Criminal Court (1998), Manual on the Effective Investigation and Documentation of Torture and Other Cruel, Inhuman or Degrading Treatment or Punishment (Istanbul Protocol) (1999).

[246] Convention against Torture and Other Cruel, Inhuman or Degrading Treatment or Punishment (adopted 10 December 1984, entered into force 26 June 1987) UNTS (CAT).

[247] Declaration on the Protection of All Persons from Being Subjected to Torture and Other Cruel, Inhuman or Degrading Treatment or Punishment (adopted 9 December 1975, entered into force 26 June 1987).

The definition of torture in the Torture Declaration was considered not to be precise enough and was criticized on various points. The discussions resulted in a more elaborate and more complex definition which appears in Article 1 of the CAT.[248]

In addition, the CAT prohibits derogation from the prohibition against torture in Article 2(2), providing: "No exceptional circumstances whatsoever, whether a state of war or a threat of war, internal political instability or any other public emergency, may be invoked as a justification of torture."

The duty of State to prevent torture and other ill treatment is enshrined within Articles 4 and 5 of the CAT, which obligates States to enact laws recognizing torture as a criminal offense, and take all necessary measures to establish jurisdiction over such offenses.

II. Prohibition of the Use of Torture against Arrested Terrorist Persons

The prohibition of torture, as a peremptory norm of international law, prohibits torture and any inhumane treatment against persons convicted, detained or suspected of terrorist activities. UN Secretary General Kofi Annan, in his message on Human Rights Day, placed emphasis on the prohibition of torture in the fight against terrorism and stated that: "Torture can never be an instrument to fight terror, for torture is an instrument of terror. ... The international community must speak forcefully, and with one voice, against torture in all its forms."[249]

Regarding the prohibition of the use of torture against arrested terrorist persons the Committee of Ministers of the Council of Europe absolutely prohibits the use of torture against arrested or detained for terrorist activities.[250] It states that:

> The use of torture or of inhuman or degrading treatment or punishment is absolutely prohibited, in all circumstances, and in particular during the arrest, questioning and detention of a person suspected of or convicted of terrorist

---

[248] H. Danelius, 'Convention against Torture and other Cruel, Inhumane or Degrading or Punishment' (2008) *United Nations Audiovisual Library of International Law*, http://untreaty.un.org/cod/avl/pdf/ha/catcidtp/catcidtp_e.pdf [23 July 2013].

[249] Kofi Annan the United Nations Secretary General, 'Message on Human Rights Day', Department of Public Information, News and Media Division, New York, 10 December 2005.

[250] Council of Europe Guidelines on Human Rights and the Fight against Terrorism, IV.

activities, irrespective of the nature of the acts that the person is suspected of or for which he/she was convicted.

i. Chahal v United Kingdom

The ECtHR in 1996 regarding the case of *Chahal v United Kingdom*,[251] No 22414/93 concerned the UK government's attempt to deport Mr. Chahal, an Indian national of Sikh origin, to India on the grounds that his alleged involvement in Sikh separatist activities constituted a threat to the national security of the UK.

The ECtHR, in *Chahal v the United Kingdom*, highlights the absolute prohibition of torture and other inhumane and degrading treatments, and emphasizes on the prohibition of returning the persons at risk of torture to their countries as follows:

> The Court is well aware of the difficulties faced by states in modern times in protecting their communities from terrorist violence. However, even in these circumstances, the Convention prohibits in absolute terms torture or inhuman or degrading treatment or punishment, irrespective of the victim's conduct.[252]

c) Prohibition of Torture and Cruel, Inhuman or Degrading Treatment or Punishment within International Humanitarian Law in Counter-terrorism Measures

Beside the IHRL conventions on the prohibition of torture and inhumane treatment, IHL conventions contain provisions prohibiting inhumane treatment against persons in armed conflicts. For example, Geneva Convention I for the Amelioration of the Condition of the Wounded and Sick in Armed Forces in the Field, 12 August 1949;[253] Geneva Convention II for the Amelioration of the Condition of Wounded, Sick and Shipwrecked Members of Armed Forces at Sea, 12 August 1949;[254] and Geneva

---

[251] *Chahal v United Kingdom* [1996] No 22414/93 (European Court of Human Rights, 15 November 1996) http://hudoc.echr.coe.int/sites/eng/pages/search.aspx?i=001-58004 [20 December 2012].

[252] *Chahal v United Kingdom*, paragraph 79.

[253] Geneva Convention I for the Amelioration of the Condition of the Wounded and Sick in Armed Forces in the Field (adopted 12 August 1949, entered into fore 21 October 1951) UNTS (First Geneva Convention), Art 3 (1).

[254] Geneva Convention for the Amelioration of the Condition of Wounded, Sick and Shipwrecked Members of Armed Forces at Sea (adopted 12 August 1949, entered into fore 21 October 1951) UNTS (Second Geneva Convention) Art 3 (1).

Convention III relative to the Treatment of Prisoners of War, 12 August 1949[255] include cruel treatments and torture in the list of prohibited acts.

I. Prohibition of Torture within International Humanitarian Law Instruments

Terrorism is prohibited within Article 33 of the Geneva Convention IV relative to the Protection of Civilian Persons in Time of War of 12 August 1949. Article 33 of the Convention provides: "No protected person may be punished for an offence he or she has not personally committed. Collective penalties and likewise all measures of intimidation or of terrorism are prohibited."

Article 32 of the Geneva Convention Relative to Protection of Civilian Persons in Time of War emphasizes the prohibition against any physical suffering, torture and corporal punishment. The provision elaborates upon the prohibition as follows:

> The High Contracting Parties specifically agree that each of them is prohibited from taking any measure of such a character as to cause the physical suffering or extermination of protected persons in their hands. This prohibition applies not only to murder, torture, corporal punishments, mutilation and medical or scientific experiments not necessitated by the medical treatment of a protected person, but also to any other measures of brutality whether applied by civilian or military agents.

Article 75 (2) Additional Protocol I to the Geneva Conventions of 12 August 1949 relating to the Protection of Victims of International Armed Conflicts of 8 June 1977 prohibits the use of violence and terror against civilians.

Article 75(2) (a), that prohibits certain actions of civilians or military agents anywhere and in any circumstances, reads as follows:

> "(a) violence to the life, health, or physical or mental well-being of persons, in particular: i. murder; ii. torture of all kinds, whether physical or mental; iii. corporal punishment; and iv. mutilation."[256]

---

[255] Geneva Convention Relative to the Treatment of Prisoners of War ((adopted 12 August 1949, entered into fore 21 October 1951) UNTS (Third Geneva Convention) Art 3 (1).

[256] Protocol Additional to the Geneva Conventions of 12 August 1949, and relating to the Protection of Victims of International Armed Conflicts (adopted 8 June 1979, entered into force 7 December 1979) UNTS (Protocol I), Art 75 (2) (a).

Additional Protocol II to the Geneva Conventions of 12 August 1949 relating to the Protection of Victims of Non-International Armed Conflicts of 8 June 1977 prohibits terrorism in all non-international armed conflicts alongside any degrading and "cruel treatments" such as "torture" and "corporal punishment":

> The following acts against the persons referred to in paragraph I are and shall remain prohibited at any time and in any place whatsoever:
>
> (a) violence to the life, health and physical or mental well-being of persons, in particular murder as well as cruel treatment such as torture, mutilation or any form of corporal punishment; (b)collective punishments; (c) taking of hostages; (d) acts of terrorism; (e) outrages upon personal dignity, in particular humiliating and degrading treatment, rape, enforced prostitution and any form or indecent assault; (f) slavery and the slave trade in all their forms; (g) pillage; (h) threats to commit any or the foregoing acts.[257]

The Inter-American Convention to Prevent and Punish Torture defines torture in Article 2 as any inflicted physical or mental pain or suffering on a person. The Convention further elaborates upon the definition of torture in the following terms:

> Torture shall be understood to be any act intentionally performed whereby physical or mental pain or suffering is inflicted on a person for purposes of criminal investigation, as a means of intimidation, as personal punishment, as a preventive measure, as a penalty, or for any other purpose. Torture shall also be understood to be the use of methods upon a person intended to obliterate the personality of the victim or to diminish his physical or mental capacities, even if they do not cause physical pain or mental anguish. The concept of torture shall not include physical or mental pain or suffering that is inherent in or solely the consequence of lawful measures, provided that they do not include the performance of the acts or use of the methods referred to in this article.[258]

II. The Use of Torture and Degrading Treatment in the Interrogations of Terrorist Suspects Following September 11

Practices of torture against those detained in counter-terrorism operations are not a new phenomenon. Following September 11, the US sought to circumvent its international obligations with respect to torture and ill-treatment in the interrogation of terrorist suspects. In late 2005, the US Congress passed the Detainee Treatment Act

---

[257] Protocol Additional to the Geneva Conventions of 12 August 1949, and relating to the Protection of Victims of Non-International Armed Conflicts (adopted 8 June 1979, entered into force 7 December 1979) UNTS (Protocol II), Art 4 (2) (d).

[258] Inter-American Convention to Prevent and Punish Torture (adopted 9 December 1985, entered into force 28 February 1987) OASTS (IACPPT).

that explicitly prohibited the use of ill-treatment by US officials. Later, President Bush attached a statement indicating that he intended to reserve the right to waive the provision if he considers it necessary to prevent further terrorist attacks. This law was signed by President Bush on October 2006. A set of revised army interrogation rules were adopted in September 2006 that explicitly prohibited a number of previously approved interrogation techniques, including forced nudity or sexual acts and simulated drowning known as "water-boarding." These rules do, however, not apply to intelligence services and President Bush has openly defended the continued use of "alternative procedures" by the CIA in the interrogation of terrorist suspects.[259]

International human rights NGOs have reported widespread and systematic abuse against detainees held in US custody in Iraq, Afghanistan and at Guantanamo Bay. Moreover, concerns exist that numerous terrorist suspects have been detained in secret detention facilities operated by the US for the specific purpose of being interrogated through abusive methods.[260] For instance, the use of torture and other abuse by US personnel abroad was far more pervasive than revealed in the Abu Ghraib photos and extended to numerous US detention facilities in Afghanistan, Iraq and at Guantnamo Bay.[261]

The Committee against Torture (CAT Committee), following September 11, issued a statement on 22 November 2001. Within this general statement the Committee highlights the non-derogable nature of prohibitions against torture, stating:

> The Committee against Torture reminds State parties to the Convention of the non-derogable nature of most of the obligations undertaken by them in ratifying the Convention. The obligations contained in Articles 2 (whereby "no exceptional circumstances whatsoever may be invoked as a justification of torture"), 15 (prohibiting confessions extorted by torture being admitted in evidence, except against the torturer), and 16 (prohibiting cruel, inhuman or degrading treatment or punishment) are three such provisions and must be observed in all circumstances.[262]

---

[259] International Helsinki Federation for Human Rights, 'Counter-terrorism measures and the prohibition on torture and ill-treatment, A briefing paper on developments in Europe, Central Asia and North America' (2006), p 16   http://www.UNCHR.org/refworld/category,COI,,THEMGUIDE,, 46963ae 90,0.html [27 February 2013].

[260] International Helsinki Federation for Human Rights, p 16.

[261] Human Rights Watch, 'By the Numbers' 26 April 2006 http://www.hrw.org/node/11352/ section/2 [27 February 2013].

III.   Use of Torture under the Guise of Counter-Terrorism

The following examples show the practical use of torture by States against persons under the pretext of counter-terrorism measures:

i.   The European Commission of Human Rights found five techniques that are routinely used by UK officials against Irish Republic Army (IRA) detainees, namely wall-standing; hooding; subjection to continuous hissing noise; deprivation of food; and deprivation of sleep.[263]

ii.   Argentina established 280 internment camps; and used torture and executions in its own State-terrorism against non-State militants in 1980, prior to the end of the Dirty War in 1983.[264]

iii. Torture was used against security detainees by the Algerian government during the war of independence against France and in the conflict during 1990s. [265]

iv.   Israel permits the use of sleep deprivation in interrogation.[266]

Generally, States should criminalize, investigate and prosecute any occurrence of torture or cruel inhuman or degrading treatments or punishments.[267]

III. Cruel, Inhuman or Degrading Treatments

Although torture is defined in international human rights instruments, no specific definition exists for "cruel, inhuman or degrading treatment" within international

---

[262] Office of the High Commissioner for Human Rights, 'Statement of the Committee against Torture' 22 November 2001, paragraphs 4-5 http://www.unhchr.ch/tbs/doc.nsf/0/c25a521171ce37ecc1 256b20004cc4c4?Opendocument [01 March 2013].

[263] *Ireland v. United Kingdom* [1978] 5310/71 (European Court of Human Rights 18 January 1978) , Paragraphs 96-104 http://hudoc.echr.coe.int/sites/eng/pages/search.aspx?i=001-57506#{%22it emid%22:[%22001-57506%22]} [23 July 2013].

[264] United Nations, General Assembly, Promotion and Protection of All Human Rights Civil, Political, Economic, Social and Cultural Rights including the Right to Development, Thirteenth Session, *Human Rights Council*, A/HRC/13/42, 19 February 2010 http://www2.ohchr.org/english /bodies/hrcouncil/docs/13session/A-HRC-13-42.pdf [28 February 2013].

[265] UN Committee Against Torture (CAT), Concluding observations of the Committee against Torture: Algeria,   26   May   2008,   CAT/C/DZA/CO/3,   Paragraphs   70-80 http://www.refworld.org/docid/48c637982.html [23 July 2013].

[266] *The Public Committee against Torture in Israel v. The State of Israel* [1999] HCJ 5100/94 (Supreme Court of Israel 26 May 1999) http://elyon1.court.gov.il/Files_ENG/02/690/007/A34/02007 690.A34.pdf [28 February 2013].

[267] E. Stubbins Batesand et al, *Terrorism and International Law, Accountability, Remedies, and Reforms*, pp 103-106.

human rights instruments. Article 16(1) of the CAT describes inhuman or degrading treatment as acts that do not amount to torture, such as:

> Each State Party shall undertake to prevent in any territory under its jurisdiction other acts of cruel, inhuman or degrading treatment or punishment which do not amount to torture as defined in article 1, when such acts are committed by or at the instigation of or with the consent or acquiescence of a public official or other person acting in an official capacity.

i.   Selcuk and Asker v Turkey

A family in South East Turkey complained that soldiers deliberately burned their homes while the State alleged the family was acting under the influence of the PKK to obtain money. The applicants stated that, some months earlier, the villagers had been warned by security forces that certain houses would be destroyed on the grounds that they were allegedly used by the PKK if the villagers did not leave their village. The soldiers went to the houses, which they forcibly entered and searched, telling the applicants to remove their possessions. However, while they were inside, trying to save their furniture and belongings, the villagers realized that the soldiers had set fire to the house. Villagers were prevented from attempting to extinguish the fires by the soldiers. The case was referred to the ECtHR by European Commission of Human Rights on 22 January 1997. The case called *Selcuk and Asker v Turkey*. [268]

The ECtHR accepted the facts, as found by the Commission, that the security forces were responsible for burning of the applicant's property and further categorized the destruction of the applicant's house as inhumane treatment under Article 3 of the ECHR. The actions were held to amount to a violation of Article 3 by eight votes to one on the following basis: "In view of manner in which applicants' homes destroyed and their personal circumstances, they must have been caused suffering of sufficient severity for acts of security forces to be categorized as inhuman treatment."[269]

---

[268] *Selcuk and Asker v. Turkey* [1997] 796/998-999 (European Court of Human Rights 4 April 1998) http://sim.law.uu.nl/sim/caselaw/Hof.ns f/e4ca7ef017f8c045c1256849004787f5/5fd70d076df7 a1a9c1256640004c38fb?OpenDocument [01 March 2013].
[269] *Selcuk and Asker v. Turkey*, paragraphs 72-80.

Similar to cruel and inhumane treatment, degrading treatment is not defined within international human rights instruments. However, such treatment includes all ill-treatment that may not reach the level of "inhuman". For example, it may include various measures designed to break the physical or moral resistance of the victim. The objective may simply be to humiliate and debase the person concerned.[270]

5.1.3   The Right to Fair Trial

The right to a fair trial is associated with the rule of law and the principle of equality before the law. This right is one of the most extensive human rights that has defined by various international and regional human rights instruments.

a) The Right to Fair Trial within International Human Rights Instruments

The right to a fair trial is enshrined within Article 10 of the UDHR as follows: "Everyone is entitled in full equality to a fair and public hearing by an independent and impartial tribunal, in the determination of his rights and obligations and of any criminal charge against him."

Moreover, Article 14 of the ICCPR consists of provisions about the right to a fair trial and a public hearing, providing:

> All persons shall be equal before the courts and tribunals. In the determination of any criminal charge against him, or of his rights and obligations in a suit at law, everyone shall be entitled to a fair and public hearing by a competent, independent and impartial tribunal established by law.

ACHR emphasizes the right to fair trial in Article 8 as follows:

> Every person has the right to a hearing, with due guarantees and within a reasonable time, by a competent, independent, and impartial tribunal, previously established by law, in the substantiation of any accusation of a criminal nature made against him or for the determination of his rights and obligations of a civil, labour, fiscal, or any other nature.

---

[270] Organization for Security and Co-operation in Europe (OSCE), *Countering Terrorism, Protecting Human Rights: A Manual*, p 123.

The right to a fair trial has been enshrined within Article 6 of the ECHR as: "Everyone is entitled to a fair and public hearing within a reasonable time by an independent and impartial tribunal established by law." This right has been emphasized within several other instruments and documents must be respected in administrative, civil and criminal cases. [271]

The right to a fair trial is one of the fundamental pillars of IHRL aimed towards protecting individuals from arbitrary treatment. Such provisions attempt to ensure that individuals are not wrongfully convicted or punished by the States. The right to a fair trial does not appear in the list of rights that may not be derogated from during states of emergency. The Human Rights Committee, in paragraph 2 of the General Comment No 29, mentions that the principles of legality and the rule of law require that fundamental requirements of fair trial must be respected during a state of emergency. Similarly, the IACtHR, in its Advisory Opinion of 6 October 1987, reaffirmed the Article 8 (1) of the ACHR in paragraphs 3 and 27 of its Advisory Opinion. It mentioned: "Judicial guarantees should be exercised within the framework and the principles of due process of law, expressed in Article 8 of the Convention."[272]

Both the Inter-American Commission on Human Rights in its Report on Terrorism and Human Rights on 22 October 2002,[273] and the IACtHR, in its advisory opinion of 6 October 1987 (Judicial Guarantees in States of Emergency), have stated that the principles of due process of law cannot be suspended in states of emergency.[274] The IACtHR decided that:

> Reading Article 8 together with Articles 7(6), 25 and 27(2) of the Convention leads to the conclusion that the principles of due process of law cannot be

---

[271] See, Universal Declaration of Human Rights; Convention against Torture and Other Cruel, Inhuman or Degrading Treatment or Punishment; Code of Conduct for Law Enforcement Officials; Body of Principles for the Protection of All Persons under Any Form of Detention or Imprisonment; Standard Minimum Rules for the Treatment of Prisoners; Guidelines on the Role of Prosecutors and the Basic Principles on the Role of Lawyers; the Rules of Procedure of the International Criminal Tribunals for the former Yugoslavia and Rwanda; and the Statute of the International Criminal Court; Human Rights Committee, General Comment No 32, 2007.

[272] Inter-American Court of Human Rights (IACtHR), Advisory Opinion OC-9/87, October 6, 1987, paragraph 41 (3).

[273] Inter-American Commission on Human Rights, Report on Terrorism and Human Rights, paragraphs 245 and 247.

[274] L. Doswald-Beck, *Fair Trial, Right to International Protection'*, *Max Planck Encyclopedia of public International Law*, Oxford University Press, United Kingdom, paragraphs 1,3,10,11, and 12.

suspended in states of exception insofar as they are necessary conditions for the procedural institutions regulated by the Convention to be considered judicial guarantees. This result is even clearer with respect to *habeas corpus* and *amparo*, which are indispensable for the protection of the human rights that are not subject to derogation and to which the Court will now refer.[275]

The report of the Inter-American Commission of Human Rights on Terrorism and Human Rights on 22 October 2002 emphasizes the right to a fair trial of persons accused of terrorism. It provides that the member States must guarantee to all persons accused of terrorism-related crimes the right to due process and to a fair trial, within a reasonable time, by an independent and impartial tribunal established by law.[276]

Fair trial rights are not only a fundamental safeguard to ensure that individuals are not unjustly punished under criminal law, they are also indispensable for the protection of other human rights, including the right to freedom from torture; the right to life; the right to freedom of expression; and the right to freedom of association.[277] The UN Human Rights Commission, in General Comment No 13, presents a wide area for the fair trial rights beyond the individual rights however apply entire a trial. It states that:

> The Committee notes that article 14 of the Covenant is of a complex nature and that different aspects of its provisions will need specific comments. All of these provisions are aimed at ensuring the proper administration of justice, and to this end uphold a series of individual rights such as equality before the courts and tribunals and the right to a fair and public hearing by a competent, independent and impartial tribunal established by law. Not all reports provided details on the legislative or other measures adopted specifically to implement each of the provisions of article 14.[278]

Under limited conditions, such as times of emergency, the right to a fair trial is derogable with respect to the impartiality and independence of the court. The Human Rights Committee, in General Comment No 29 on 31 August 2001, states that:

---

[275] Inter-American Court of Human Rights, Advisory Opinion on Judicial Guarantees in State of Emergency, Series A No 9, (6 October 1987), paragraph 30.

[276] Inter-American Commission on Human Rights, Report on Terrorism and Human Rights, paragraphs 261.

[277] Organization for Security and Co-operation in Europe (OSCE), *Countering Terrorism, Protecting Human Rights: A Manual*, p 165.

[278] UN Human Rights Committee (HRC), CCPR General Comment No. 13, Equality before the Courts and the Right to a Fair and Public Hearing by an Independent Court Established by Law, Art 14 (1984), paragraph 1 http://www.refworld.org/docid/453883f90.html [01 March 2013].

The fact that some of the provisions of the Covenant have been listed in Article 4 (paragraph 2), as not being subject to derogation does not mean that other articles in the Covenant may be subjected to derogations at will, even where a threat to the life of the nation exists. The legal obligation to narrow down all derogations to those strictly required by the exigencies of the situation establishes both for States parties and for the Committee a duty to conduct a careful analysis under each article of the Covenant based on an objective assessment of the actual situation.[279]

I. Basic Requirements for a Fair Trial within the Statute of the International Criminal Court

The Rome Statute of the ICC contains provisions regarding the basic requirements for a fair trial based on international criminal law, which are outlined as follows:

i.   The presumption of innocence.

ii.   The right to communicate with legal representatives freely and in confidence.

iii. Privilege against self-incrimination.

iv.   The right not to make an un-sworn oral or written statement in one's own defence.

v.   The right to remain silent without such silence being a consideration in the determination of innocence or guilt.

vi.   The right not to have imposed upon the accused any reversal of the burden of proof or onus of rebuttal.[280]

The other basic rights that are identified and associated with the right to fair trial are principle of legality;[281] equality before the law or equal treatment by the law;[282] the right to presumption of innocence;[283] the right to a hearing with due guarantees

---

[279] UN Human Rights Committee (HRC), CCPR General Comment No. 29, Derogations during a State of Emergency, Article 4 (2001), CCPR/C/21/Rev.1/Add.11 http://www.UNCHR.org/refworld/docid/453883fd1f.html [01 March 2013].

[280] Rome Statute of the International Criminal Court, Arts 67(1)(b), (g), (h), and (i).

[281] ICCPR, Art 14(1).

[282] ICCPR, Art 14(1).

[283] ICCPR, Art14(2).

and within a reasonable time by a competent, independent and impartial tribunal;[284] the right to call witnesses;[285] the right to legal assistance;[286] the right to be informed promptly in understandable language;[287] the right to adequate time for the preparation of defence and the right to access to evidence and documents;[288] and the right to appeal to a higher tribunal.[289]

b) Other Related Rights

The following paragraphs will deal with some of the most related rights that must be protected during a fair trial process and the following sections will demonstrate how these rights may be violated by counter-terrorism measures.

I. Principle of Legality

The principle of legality means that any criminal act must be recognized and defined by law and is considered to be a non-derogable right in human rights treaties.[290] The offence must be clearly defined in law, so that the individual can know from the wording of the provision what behaviour is considered criminal. If, subsequent to the commission of the offence, a provision is made by law for the imposition of a lighter penalty, the offender shall benefit from this.[291]

i.   Principle of legality within international human rights instruments

The principle of legality has been protected by various international and regional instruments such, as the UDHR; the ICCPR; and the ECHR. The UDHR, in Article 11 (2), states:

> No one shall be held guilty of any penal offence on account of any act or omission which did not constitute a penal offence, under national or international law, at the time when it was committed. Nor shall a heavier

---

[284] ICCPR, Art 14(2) (b).
[285] ICCPR, Art 14(3).
[286] ICCPR, Art 14(3).
[287] ICCPR, Article 14(3), ACHR, Art 8 (2) (b), ECHR, Art 6 (3) (a).
[288] ICCPR, Art 14(3).
[289] ICCPR, Art 14(5).
[290] ICCPR, Art 4.
[291] L. Doswald-Beck, 'Fair Trial, Right to International Protection', Max Planck Encyclopedia of public International Law, paragraphs 62-63.

penalty be imposed than the one that was applicable at the time the penal offence was committed.

Article 15 (1) of the ICCPR states:

No one shall be held guilty of any criminal offence on account of any act or omission which did not constitute a criminal offence, under national or international law, at the time when it was committed. Nor shall a heavier penalty be imposed than the one that was applicable at the time when the criminal offence was committed. If, subsequent to the commission of the offence, provision is made by law for the imposition of the lighter penalty, the offender shall benefit thereby.

The ECHR within Article 7 states:

No one shall be held guilty of any criminal offence on account of any act or omission which did not constitute a criminal offence under national or international law at the time when it was committed. Nor shall a heavier penalty be imposed than the one that was applicable at the time the criminal offence was committed.

Furthermore, Article 6 (1) ECHR provides:

In the determination of his civil rights and obligations or of any criminal charge against him, everyone is entitled to a fair and public hearing within a reasonable time by an independent and impartial tribunal established by law. Judgment shall be pronounced publicly but the press and public may be excluded from all or part of the trial in the interests of morals, public order or national security in a democratic society, where the interests of juveniles or the protection of the private life of the parties so require, or to the extent strictly necessary in the opinion of the court in special circumstances where publicity would prejudice the interests of justice.

ii.   Principle of legality and counter-terrorism measures

In relation to counter-terrorism measures, respect for the principle of legality is important because, due to the lack of a universally accepted definition of terrorism, States have taken the opportunity to prosecute and punish political opponents as "terrorists".

The Inter American Commission on Human Rights, in its Report on Human Rights and Terrorism, emphasizes the principle of legality through a narrow definition of terrorism based on the fundamental principles of criminal law such as presumption innocence to prevent any implication on criminal liability and punishment such as denial of refugee status.

The Human Rights Committee, in its Concluding Observations in 2003 on Estonia, expressed concern on the protection of the principle of legality in counter-terrorism processes. The committee states that:

> The Committee is concerned that the relatively broad definition of the crime of terrorism and of membership of a terrorist group under the State party's Criminal Code may have adverse consequences for the protection of rights under article 15 of the Covenant, a provision which significantly is non-derogable under article 4, paragraph 2.[292]

A number of the international anti-terrorism conventions consider the right to a fair trial for terrorists within their provisions. For instance, the International Convention for the Suppression of Acts of Nuclear Terrorism guarantees the right to a fair trial for the persons who are taken into custody, providing:

> Any person who is taken into custody or regarding whom any other measures are taken or proceedings are carried out pursuant to this Convention shall be guaranteed fair treatment, including enjoyment of all rights and guarantees in conformity with the law of the State in the territory of which that person is present and applicable provisions of international law, including the international law of human rights.[293]

State counter-terrorism legislation violates the rule of law's requirement for precision and prospectively. A lack of precision and excessive breadth exists in the definition of terrorism, meaning that many non-criminal actions may be criminalized as terrorism. Furthermore, excessive breadth in regulations that define the powers of law enforcement officials, armed forces, and intelligence services in counter-terrorism. In the independence of the judiciary and the rule of lawyers the counter-terrorism measures present risks by the multiple emergency laws and their overlapping regulations.[294]

---

[292] United Nations Human Rights Committee, Concluding Observations: Estonia, (15 April 2003) CCPR/CO/77/EST, C, paragraph 8: http://www.UNCHR.org/ref world /docid/3f25a0787.html [13 October 2012].

[293] International Convention for the Suppression of Acts of Nuclear Terrorism (adopted 13 April 2005, entered into force 7 July 2007) UNTS, Arts 12, 13.

[294] E. Stubbins Batesand et al, *Terrorism and International Law, Accountability, Remedies, and Reforms,* pp139-140.

iii.   Ecer and Zeyrek v Turkey

On 2 September 1993 security forces from the Sirnak central gendarmerie command apprehended Abdülaziz Ecer and Mr Mehmet Zeyrek. They had been arrested on the grounds that they were wanted for the offences of aiding and sheltering members of the PKK terrorist organization and acting as couriers in the organization as well as supplying logistic support to the organization. The applicants were then placed in custody. During their interrogation the applicants both confessed that they had been involved in the PKK since 1988 and that they had supplied food and money to PKK militants. On the same day, 23 September 1993, the applicants were brought before the Sirnak Magistrates' Court (Sulh Ceza Mahkemesi). Before the court the applicants denied their involvement in the PKK and claimed that they were innocent of the charges. The court ordered the applicants' detention on remand. The case brought to the ECtHR. In *Ecer and Zeyrek v Turkey* the applicants alleged, in particular, that their punishment occurred in breach of Article 7 of the ECHR. The ECtHR on 27 February 2001 held that there has been a violation of Article 7 (1) of the Convention and states within its judgment:

> The Court recalls that the guarantee enshrined in Article 7, which is an essential element of the rule of law, occupies a prominent place in the Convention system of protection, as is underlined by the fact that no derogation from it is permissible under Article 15 in a time of war or other public emergency. It should be construed and applied, as follows from its object and purpose, in such a way as to provide effective safeguards against arbitrary prosecution, conviction and punishment.[295]

II. Equality before the Law (Legal Equality or Prohibition of Discrimination)

Firstly, the principle of equality before the courts means that every person appearing before a court has the right not to be discriminated against either in the course of the proceedings or in the way the law is applied to the person concerned, irrespective of one's gender, race, origin or financial status. Further, whether individuals are suspected of crimes, the rights have to be equally secured to everyone. Secondly, the principle of equality means that all persons must have equal access to the courts.[296]

---

[295] *Ecer and Zeyrek v. Turkey* [2001] 29295/95, 29363/95 (European Court of Human Rights 27 February 200) , paragraph 29.
[296] United Nations. Office of the High Commissioner for Human Rights, International Bar Association, 'Human Rights in the Administration of Justice: A Manual on Human Rights for Judges, Prosecutors and Lawyers', 2003, p 218 www.ohchr.org/Documents/Publications/training9Titleen.pdfd

The prohibition of discrimination stands at the centre of human rights law and is recognized as *jus cogens*. The Committee on the Elimination of Racial Discrimination (CERD), in General Recommendation No 30,[297] called on States to ensure that any measures taken in the fight against terrorism do not discriminate, in purpose or effect, on the grounds of race, colour, descent, or national or ethnic origin.[298]

i.   Equality before the law within international human rights instruments

The right to equality before the law is protected by the UDHR, ICCPR, ACHR and other regional and international instruments and documents.[299]

The UDHR emphasizes the principle of equality before the law in Article 7. It provides: "All are equal before the law and are entitled without any discrimination to equal protection of the law. All are entitled to equal protection against any discrimination in violation of this Declaration and against any incitement to such discrimination."

In addition, Article 26 of the ICCPR provides:

> All persons are equal before the law and are entitled without any discrimination to the equal protection of the law. In this respect, the law shall prohibit any discrimination and guarantee to all persons equal and effective protection against discrimination on any ground such as race, colour, sex,

---

[13 October 2012].

[297] United Nations Committee on the Elimination of Racial Discrimination, General Recommendation No.30 Discrimination Against Non Citizens, Office of the High Commissioner for Human Rights http://www.unhchr.ch/tbs/doc.nsf/%28Symbol%29/e3980a673769e229c1256f8d0057 cd3d?Opendocument [23 July 2013].

[298] United Nations Committee on the Elimination of Racial Discrimination, General Recommendation No.30, paragraph 6.

[299] See, Articles 1, 2 and 7 of the Universal Declaration of Human Rights; articles 2(1), (3), 4(1) of the International Covenant on Civil and Political Rights; article 2(2) of the International Covenant on Economic, Social and Cultural Rights; articles 2, 3, 18(3) and 28 of the African Charter on Human and Peoples' Rights; articles 1, and 27(1) of the American Convention on Human Rights; article 14 of the European Convention on Human Rights; articles 2 and 15 of the 1979 Convention on the Elimination of All Forms of Discrimination against Women; article 2 of the 1989 Convention on the Rights of the Child; and the 1966 International Convention on the Elimination of All Forms of Racial Discrimination. Of the four 1949 Geneva Conventions, Articles 3 and 27 of the Geneva Convention relative to the Protection of Civilian Persons in Time of War; articles 9(1) and 75(1) of the 1977 Protocol Additional to the Geneva Conventions of 12 August 1949, and relating to the Protection of Victims of International Armed Conflicts (Protocol I); and articles 2(1) and 4(1) of the 1977 Protocol Additional to the Geneva Conventions of 12 August 1949, and relating to the Protection of Victims of Non-International Armed Conflicts (Protocol II).

language, religion, political or other opinion, national or social origin, property, birth or other status.

Moreover, Article 24 of the ACHR consists of provisions on the principle of equality before the law.

The US counter-terrorism and security measures since September 11, 2001 have a disproportionate effect on Arabs, Muslims and others of certain national origins. The US security measures involve not only detention, but also interviews, registration and databases on foreign nationals containing information on thousands of Arabs and Muslims.[300]

III. Right to be Presumed Innocent

The right to be presumed innocent means that persons are considered innocent until proven guilty. The presumption of innocence serves to ensure that the prosecution of an individual must prove each element of the offense beyond a reasonable doubt (or some other level of proof depending on the criminal justice system) and that the accused bears no burden of proof.[301]

The Human Rights Committee, in General Comment No 13, emphasizes that the principle of presumption of innocence means the burden of proof of the charge is on the prosecution and the accused has the benefit of the doubt.[302]

i. Right to be presumed innocent within international human rights instruments

This right is recognized by Article 11(1) UDHR; Article 14(2) ICCPR; Article 8(2) ACHR; Article 6 (2) ECHR; Article 7(1) (b) African Charter on Human and Peoples' Rights (Banjul Charter); and other international and regional documents.[303]

The UDHR contains of provision, which has recognized the right to be presumed innocent of persons. Article 11 (1) provides: "Everyone charged with a

---

[300] D. Cassel, 'International Human Rights and the United States Response to 11 September', pp 291-292.

[301] C. B. Muelle et al, *Evidence: Practice under Rules*, New York, Wolters Kluwer, 1999, pp 169-171.

[302] UN Human Rights Committee (HRC), CCPR General Comment No. 13, paragraph 7.

[303] See, Article 20(3) of the Statute of the International Criminal Tribunal for Rwanda, Article 21(3) of the Statute of the International Criminal Tribunal for the former Yugoslavia, and Article 66(1) of the Statute of the International Criminal Court.

penal offence has the right to be presumed innocent until proved guilty according to law in a public trial at which he has had all the guarantees necessary for his defence."

In addition Article 14 (2) of the ICCPR reads as follows: " Everyone charged with a criminal offence shall have the right to be presumed innocent until proved guilty according to law."

ii.   Heaney and McGuinness v Ireland

On 23 October 1990, a large explosion occurred at a British Army Royal Ulster Constabulary checkpoint in County Derry. Five British soldiers and one civilian were killed and a number of other British army personnel were seriously injured. On 24 October 1990, the police entered a house and found an assortment of gloves (rubber and knitted), balaclavas, caps and other clothing. The seven men in the house, including the owner and the applicants, were arrested and detained by the police under section 30 of the Offences against the State Act 1939 ("the 1939 Act"). It was suspected that the bombing had been carried out by the IRA and the applicants were, in turn, suspected by the police of membership of that organization and of involvement in the bombing. Two of arrested persons refused to answer any police questions. Both applicants were sentenced to six months imprisonment. The applicants then appealed to the Court of Criminal Appeal and submitted that the Special Criminal Court had erred in finding that the applicants were not confused as a result of the caution about their right to remain silent. Their application was rejected. The case was brought to the ECtHR on 17 January 1997 in the case of *Heaney and McGuinness v Ireland*. The Court held on 21 December 2000 that:

> The Court is not, therefore, called upon in the present case to consider the impact on the rights to silence or against self-incrimination of the direct or indirect use made in later proceedings against an accused of statements made pursuant to section 52 of the 1939 Act. Accordingly, the Court finds that the "degree of compulsion" imposed on the applicants by the application of section 52 of the 1939 Act with a view to compelling them to provide information relating to charges against them under that Act in effect destroyed the very essence of their privilege against self-incrimination and their right to remain silent. The Government contended that section 52 of the 1939 Act is, nevertheless, a proportionate response to the subsisting terrorist and security threat given the need to ensure the proper administration of justice and the maintenance of public order and peace.[304]

iii.   **Right to hearing by a competent, independent and impartial tribunal**

This right is enshrined within the UDHR[305], the ICCPR[306], the ACHR[307] and the ECHR.[308]

The UDHR emphases on the right of the persons hearing by a competence, independent and impartial tribunal. Article 10 provides: "Everyone is entitled in full equality to a fair and public hearing by an independent and impartial tribunal, in the determination of his rights and obligations and of any criminal charge against him."

Furthermore, Article 14 (1) states: "...everyone shall be entitled to a fair and public hearing by a competent, independent and impartial tribunal established by law."

iv.   **Prohibition of trial of civilians in military and special tribunals: The Human Rights Committee critiques**

The Human Rights Committee, in General Comment 32, states that the trial of civilians in military or special courts may raise serious problems as far as the equitable, impartial and independent administration of justice is concerned. The Committee notes:

> While the Covenant does not prohibit the trial of civilians in military or special courts, it requires that such trials are in full conformity with the requirements of article 14 and that its guarantees cannot be limited or modified because of the military or special character of the court concerned. The Committee also notes that the trial of civilians in military or special courts may raise serious problems as far as the equitable, impartial and independent administration of justice is concerned.[309]

Special security courts and military tribunals, including those trying alleged offences by military personnel, must respect the same requirements of independence

---

[304] *Heaney and McGuinness v. Ireland* [2000] No. 34720/97 (European Court of Human Rights 21 December 2000), paragraphs 54-57 http://hudoc.echr.coe.int/sites/eng/pages/search.aspx ?i=001-59097 [1 March 2013].

[305] UDHR, Art 10.

[306] ICCPR Art 14(1).

[307] ACHR, Art 8(1).

[308] ECHR, Art 6(1).

[309] UN Human Rights Committee (HRC), CCPR General Comment No. 32, paragraph 22.

and impartiality as civilian tribunals. Treaty bodies increasingly opine that military tribunals should not try civilians.[310]

v.   Castillo Petruzzi v. Peru

The trial of a person accused of terrorist acts must take place with respect to structural and procedural guarantees inherent in the notion of a fair trial. First, the court must be independent and impartial. This right has been violated on some occasions. For example, the IACtHR, in *Castillo Petruzzi v. Peru*, confirmed the use of a military court violated the right to a hearing by an independent and impartial tribunal. On 15 October 1993, Jaime Francisco Castillo-Petruzzi, Maria Concepcion Pincheira-Saez, Lautaro Enrique Mellado-Saavedra and Alejandro Astorga-Valdez were detained by members of the National Anti-Terrorism Bureau and three of them were convicted as "perpetrators of the crime of treason against the fatherland, with a sentence of life imprisonment without parole, continuous solitary confinement for the first year of the sentence and then forced labor" by the Special Military Investigative Judge of the Peruvian Air Force. This case was submitted to the IACtHR by the Inter-American Commission on Human Rights on July 22, 1997. According to the application, Peru violated the right to nationality of them by trying and convicting them of the crime of "treason against the fatherland." In 30 May 1999 the IACtHR accepted the Commission's argument and held that:

> The Commission argued that in the military court proceedings the State
> violated the following rights and guarantees of due process of law
> contemplated in the American Convention: the right to a hearing by an
> independent and impartial tribunal Article 8(1). [311]

vi.   The United States Military Order 13 November 2001

President Bush, on 13 November 2001, issued an executive order providing authorization to use military commissions to try captured individual terrorism suspects by the US. Such trials did not include any procedural safeguards to protect the rights of the accused.[312] The Military Order 2001 on Detention, Treatment and

---

[310] L. Doswald-Beck,'Fair Trial, Right to International Protection', Max Planck Encyclopedia of public International Law, paragraphs 22-23.

[311] *Castillo Petruzzi v. Peru* [1999] Ser. C. No 41 (Inter American Court of Human Rights 30 May 1999), paragraph 123 http://graduateinstitute.ch/faculty/clapham/hrdoc/docs/IACtHRpetruzzicase .html [01 March 2013].

Trial of Certain Non-citizens in the War against Terror authorizes the detention and trial of terrorists; and uses a broad definition of individuals subject to this order. Trials before military commissions do not comply with the essential fair trial safeguards or guarantees of an independent judiciary. As such, trials before military commissions are considered violations of international human rights standards.[313]

The Military Order authorized the military commissions to sit anywhere and at any time, including within the US, to prosecute individuals for violations of the laws of war and other applicable laws relating to acts of international terrorism. This was an exclusive jurisdiction. The Military Order did not apply to US citizens and applied only after the president confirmed in writing that the individual was either a member of the Al-Qaeda organization[314] that had engaged, aided, and abetted,[315] or conspired to commit acts of international terrorism;[316] or had knowingly harboured international terrorist or terrorists.[317]

One argument that supported the existence of military commissions was that the war against terrorism continued. The situation is strikingly similar to the wars on drugs, crime and poverty announced by the US governments in the past. However, maintaining the situation of a "State of war" is considered to be a serious risk to liberty in the US.[318]

The UN Human Rights Committee stated that the Article 14 of the ICCPR permits the trial of civilians by special military courts. The Committee concluded that although the ICCPR does not prohibit military tribunals, "the trying of civilians by such courts should be very exceptional and take place under condition and full guarantees of Article 14 of the ICCPR.[319] Such as right to be informed promptly and

---

[312] L. A. Dickinson, 'Using legal process to fight terrorism: detentions, military commissions, international tribunals, and the rule of law' (2002) 75 *Southern California Law Review*, p 140.

[313] P. Hoffman, 'Human Rights and Terrorism', pp 941-942.

[314] Section 2 (a) (1) (i), Military Order 2001.

[315] Section 2 (a) (1) (ii), Military Order 2001.

[316] Section 2 (a) (1) (iii), Military Order 2001.

[317] D. A. Mundis, 'The Use of Military Commissions to Prosecute Individuals Accused of Terrorist Acts' (2002) 96 (2) *The American Journal of International Law*, p 321.

[318] D. F. Vagts, 'Which Court Should Try Persons Accused of Terrorism' (2003) 14 (2) *European Journal of International Law (EJIL)* p 320.

[319] D. A. Mundis, 'The Use of Military Commissions to Prosecute Individuals Accused of Terrorist Acts', p 325.

in detail, to have adequate time and facilities for the preparation of his defence, to be tried without undue delay and some other conditions.

By mid-year 2003, military commissions had not yet been used. However, six prisoners were declared eligible for trial by such commissions in early July 2003. Nonetheless, the commissions remain authorized and may impose punishments up to that of death or life imprisonment. Later, the President's orders excluded civilian judicial review in any form. The blanket of exclusion of judicial review violates not only the right of appeal under Article 14 (5) of the ICCPR, but also the right of access to a court to challenge the lawfulness of detention under Article 9 (4), which is deemed a non-derogable right even during a time of war.[320]

IV. Right to Call Witnesses; and Access Legal Assistance, Evidence and Documents

Witnesses must normally be able to be cross-examined during public proceedings. However, exceptions are possible, including an anonymous testimony, provided that the exceptions do not infringe upon the rights of the defence and a conviction is not based to a decisive extent on such testimony.[321]

i. Right to call witnesses; and access legal assistance, evidence and documents within international instruments

These rights are considered guarantees for defendants in criminal proceedings. The right to examine witnesses is protected by international and regional human rights instruments such as the ICCPR[322], ACHR[323], ECHR[324] and other documents.

The ICCPR emphasizes on these rights in Article 14 (3) (e), (f), and (g). It provides:

---

[320] D. Cassel, 'International Human Rights and the United States Response to 11 September', pp 268-269.
[321] L. Doswald-Beck,'Fair Trial, Right to International Protection', Max Planck Encyclopedia of public International Law, paragraph 52.
[322] ICCPR, Art 14(3)(e).
[323] ACHR, Art 8(2)(f).
[324] ECHR, Art 6(d).

(e)To examine, or have examined, the witnesses against him and to obtain the attendance and examination of witnesses on his behalf under the same conditions as witnesses against him; (f) To have the free assistance of an interpreter if he cannot understand or speak the language used in court; (g) Not to be compelled to testify against himself or to confess guilt.

The ACHR recognized the right of accused to using legal counsel at trial. Article 8 (2) and (4) ACHR recognized the right of the accused to defend himself personally or to be assisted by legal counsel of his own choosing and to communicate freely and privately with his counsel.

The ECHR regarding the right of the persons to access other legal assistance in Article 6 (e) emphasizes on the right to have the free assistance of an interpreter if he cannot understand or speak the language used in court as minimum rights for everyone charged with a criminal offence.

The UNCRC within Article 37 (d) emphasizes on the right to access legal assistance for the children deprived of his or her liberty. It reads as follows:

Every child deprived of his or her liberty shall have the right to prompt access to legal and other appropriate assistance, as well as the right to challenge the legality of the deprivation of his or her liberty before a court or other competent, independent and impartial authority, and to a prompt decision on any such action.

The Human Rights Committee, in General Comments No 13, emphasizes on the right to access legal assistance, a lawyer and an interpreter during a trial.[325] Furthermore, Article 14(3) of the ICCPR provides for "adequate time and facilities for the preparation of his defence and to communicate with counsel of his own choosing." The Human Rights Committee emphasizes the right to access adequate facilities during a trial as follows: "To include access to documents and other evidence which the accused requires to prepare his case, as well as the opportunity to engage and communicate with counsel."[326] The Council of Europe, in its Guidelines on Human Rights and Fights against Terrorism, recognized the restrictions on the right to access documents as the right of accused to access to the case-file.[327]

---

[325] UN Human Rights Committee (HRC), CCPR General Comment No 13, paragraph 11.
[326] UN Human Rights Committee (HRC), CCPR General Comment No 13, paragraph 9.
[327] Council of Europe Guideline on Human Rights and Fights against Terrorism, IX (3) (ii).

In the investigation and prosecution of terrorist crimes, the Inter-American Commission on Human Rights, in the Report on Terrorism and Human Rights, called upon States to protect the judges and witnesses. The Commission argued that:

> The investigation and prosecution of terrorist crimes may render judges and other officials involved in the administration of justice vulnerable to threats. States are obliged to take all necessary measures to prevent violence against such persons. Accordingly, states may be compelled by the exigencies of a particular situation to develop mechanisms to protect a judge's life, physical integrity and independence. As in the case of threatened witnesses, however, each situation must be carefully evaluated on its own merits within the context of a particular justice system must be subject to such measures as are necessary to ensure a defendant's right to challenge the competence, independence or impartiality of his or her prosecuting tribunal, and may in no case serve to compromise a defendant's right to fundamental fairness.[328]

ii.   Doorson v The Netherlands

The ECtHR, in *Doorson v The Netherlands,* accepted the use of anonymous testimony in serious crimes to protect the life of witnesses. Desire Doorson was arrested on suspicion of having committed drug offences. A number of drug users, including six who remain anonymous, had identified him to the police as a drug dealer. In the course of a preliminary investigation two anonymous witnesses were heard by an investigating judge and their anonymous testimonies were accepted by the court. The case was referred to the ECtHR by the European Commission of Human Rights on 8 December 1994 on the basis that the right to a fair trial guaranteed under Article 6 of the ECHR may have been violated. The ECtHR held that no violation of Article 6 (3) (d) had occurred by seven votes to two on 26 March 1996, because the Court could not hold in the abstract that evidence given by a witness in open court and on oath should always be relied on in preference to other statements made by the same witness in the course of criminal proceedings, not even when the two were in conflict.[329]

The right to access to the service of a lawyer by his own choosing; the right to free access to the assistance of an interpreter when the accused cannot understand the

---

[328] Inter-American Commission on Human Rights, Report on Terrorism and Human Rights, paragraph 252.

[329] *Doorson v. The Netherlands* [1996] No 20524/92 (European Court of Human Rights 26 March 1996), http://sim.law.uu.nl/sim/caselaw/Hof.nsf/2422ec00f1ace923c1256681002b47f1/937bf8 1e_6568795fc1256640004c2f5a?OpenDocument [02 March 2013].

language used in proceeding; and the right to access evidence and documents are considered necessary means of defence and must be respected by the States' authorities.

The right to access the service of a lawyer is enshrined within the international and regional human rights instruments. For example, Article 8(2) (e) of the ACHR provides:

> "The inalienable right to be assisted by counsel provided by the state, paid or not as the domestic law provides, if the accused does not defend himself personally or engage his own counsel within the time period established by law."

iii. The right to access to the service of a lawyer: The Human Rights Committee critiques

The Human Rights Committee recognizes on the right of persons to request a person as a lawyer by his choice in General Comment 13. [330]

The Human Rights Committee challenged the violation of the right to access a lawyer in the courts under the UK Terrorism Act 2000 due to provisions concerning arrest without warrant. The Act limited this right during the first 48 hours of detention. The Committee stated:

> The Committee notes with concern that, under the general Terrorism Act 2000, suspects may be detained for 48 hours without access to a lawyer if the police suspect that such access would lead, for example, to interference with evidence or alerting another suspect. Particularly in circumstances where these powers have not been used in England and Wales for several years, where their compatibility with articles 9 and 14 inter alia is suspect, and where other less intrusive means for achieving the same ends exist, the Committee considers that the State party has failed to justify these powers. [331]

iv. Permission of restrictions: The Council of Europe position

In contrast, the Council of Europe Guidelines on human rights and the fight against terrorism justified some restrictions to the right to access and contact counsel based

---

[330] UN Human Rights Committee (HRC), CCPR General Comment No 13, paragraph 9.
[331] United Nations, Human Rights Committee, Concluding Observations of the Human Rights Committee: United Kingdom and UK Overseas Territories, (6 December 2001), CCPR/CO/73/UK, paragraph 19 http://www.refworld.org/docid/3cbbec3d2.html [23 July 2013].

on the nature of terrorism crimes.[332] The view of the Council of Europe is considered as a violation against the right of the person to access the legal counsel in a trial.

Even though the Guidelines emphasize the proportionality of the restrictions of the right to access legal counsel, Article IX states:

> Such restrictions to the right of defence must be strictly proportionate to their purpose, and compensatory measures to protect the interests of the accused must be taken so as to maintain the fairness of the proceedings and to ensure that procedural rights are not drained of their substance.[333]

V. Right to Appeal

The right to appeal to a higher tribunal must include at least one appeal on both facts and law, and not only law. The right of appeal presupposes that a written reasoned judgment was delivered by the court of earlier instance, even if such a court was itself an appellate court.[334]

i.   Right to appeal within international instruments

Human right treaties and conventions protect the right to appeal under their provisions. For instance, the right to appeal has been enshrined within the Article 14(5) of the ICCPR; Article 8(2) (8) of the ACHR; Article 2 of the ECHR; and Protocol No 7 of the ECHR.

Article 14 (5) states: "Everyone convicted of a crime shall have the right to his conviction and sentence being reviewed by a higher tribunal according to law."

ii.   Right to appeal at risk: The United States Military Order

In regard to terrorist crimes, following September 11, the right to appeal was limited in the US judicial system. For instance Section 412 (B) (3) of the PATRIOT Act violates the right to appeal and states:

---

[332] Council of Europe, Guidelines on Human Rights and the Fight against Terrorism IX (3) (i).

[333] Council of Europe, Guidelines on Human Rights and the Fight against Terrorism IX (4).

[334] L. Doswald-Beck, 'Fair Trial, Right to International Protection', Max Planck Encyclopedia of public International Law, paragraphs 57-58.

... before a circuit or district judge, the final order shall be subject to review, on appeal, by the United States Court of Appeals for the District of Columbia Circuit. There shall be no right of appeal in such proceedings to any other circuit court of appeals.

In addition, the US Military Order violates the right to appeal of the accused because it prevents individuals from seeking any direct or indirect remedies in domestic, foreign or international courts or tribunals. Section 7 (b) 2 of the US Military Order provides:

> The individual shall not be privileged to seek any remedy or maintain any proceeding, directly or indirectly, or to have any such remedy or proceeding sought on the individual's behalf, in (i) any court of the United States, or any State thereof, (ii) any court of any foreign nation, or (iii) any international tribunal.

Furthermore, the Military Order violates the right to appeal to a higher tribunal by recognizing that the Secretary of Defence as the highest authority for appeal for decisions made by the Military Commission. Sec 4 (c) (8) states: "Submission of the record of the trial, including any conviction or sentence, for review and final decision by me or by the Secretary of Defence if so designated by me for that purpose."

Generally, respect for the right to fair trial and other related rights is important because of the nature of terrorist crimes and the serious nature of potential punishments, which include capital punishment or life imprisonment.

5.1.4   The Right to Liberty and Security

The right to liberty is only concerned with physical liberty and the right to security does not mean protection from attacks by others. This will occur when a law enforcement officer obliges a person to stay somewhere or to go elsewhere, and when there is any loss of liberty. Compulsion is required even if surrender is voluntary.[335]

All human beings have the right to security and all governments have a responsibility to ensure and protect this right. The right to security is not an absolute

---

[335] Organization for Security and Co-operation in Europe (OSCE), *Countering Terrorism, Protecting Human Rights: A Manual*, p 151.

right in theory and reality, but there will always need to balance between liberty and security. Indeed, the development and implementation of IHRL and IHL standards depends on such a balance. A threat of violence always exists in society and, during the last sixty years, the international human rights framework has not been an obstacle to governments that legitimately respond to such threats and actions.[336]

All persons are protected against the unlawful or arbitrary interference with their liberty, and it is applicable in the context of criminal proceedings.[337] The right to security and liberty are discussed under the prohibition of arbitrary arrest and detention.

a) Right to liberty and security within international instruments

These rights have been protected within the provisions of the Article 9 of the UDHR; Article 9 of the ICCPR; Article 15 of the ACHR; Article 5 of the ECHR; and other international human rights instruments.[338]

The right to liberty is protected in Article 9 of the UDHR as: "No one shall be subjected to arbitrary arrest, detention or exile." Furthermore, Article 9 (1) of the ICCPR states:

> 1. Everyone has the right to liberty and security of person. No one shall be subjected to arbitrary arrest or detention. No one shall be deprived of his liberty except on such grounds and in accordance with such procedure as are established by law.

The Council of Europe, in the Guideline on Human Rights and Fight against Terrorism of 11 July 2002, emphasizes the rights of persons who are deprived of liberty for terrorist activities.[339] The Guidelines, however, allow for the following additional restrictions of liberty in light of the nature of the suspected offence:

---

[336] P. Hoffman, 'Human Rights and Terrorism', pp 949-950.
[337] Office of the United Nations High Commissioner for Human Rights (OHCHR), 'Human Rights, Terrorism and Counter-Terrorism', Factsheet, No 32, p 36.
[338] See, Article 37 of the United Nations Convention on the Rights of the Child (UNCRC), Human Rights Committee General Comments No 8, 1982, Right to Liberty and Security, and Article 6 of the African Charter on Human and People's Rights (ACHPR).
[339] Council of Europe Guideline on Human Rights and Fights against Terrorism, IX.

The imperatives of the fight against terrorism may nevertheless require that a person deprived of his/her liberty for terrorist activities be submitted to more severe restrictions than those applied to other prisoners, in particular with regard to: (i) the regulations concerning communications and surveillance of correspondence, including that between counsel and his/her client; (ii) placing persons deprived of their liberty for terrorist activities in specially secured quarters; (iii) the separation of such persons within a prison or among different prisons, on condition that the measure taken is proportionate to the aim to be achieved.[340]

b) Other Related Rights

The right to liberty and security of the person is comprised of several rights and prohibitions that will be discussed in the following paragraphs.

I. Prohibition of Arbitrary Arrest and Detention

The UNDHR, ICCPR, ECHR, ACHR and ACHPR contains of provisions on the prohibition of arbitrary detention and arrest.[341] This right may be restricted in special circumstances by observing the conditions of necessity, proportionality and non-discrimination. Therefore, the prohibition against arbitrary arrest and detention is considered a derogable right. Yet, the Human Rights Committee states that certain elements of the prohibition against arbitrary arrest and detention are non-derogable, such as the right to initiate proceedings in court, without delay, concerning the lawfulness of the detention.[342]

II. Requirement of Establishment by Law of any Deprivation of Liberty

Article 9(1) of the ICCPR; Article 5(1) of the ECHR; Article 7(2) of the ACHR; and Article 6 of the ACHPR contains provisions concerning the establishment by law of any deprivation of liberty.

According to Article 5 (1) (a), (b), and (f), detention is justifiable only in instances involving detention following conviction; detention to enforce court orders or to fulfil an obligation prescribed by law; detention following arrest to bring the individual before the competent legal authorities; detention of children for educational

---

[340] Council of Europe, in the Guideline on Human Rights and Fight against Terrorism, XI (2).
[341] ICCPR, Art 9 (1); ECHR, Art 5 (1); ACHR, Art 7 (3); and ACHPR, Art 6.
[342] UN Human Rights Committee (HRC), CCPR, General Comment No 29, paragraph 16.

supervision or to bring them before the competent legal authorities; detention of alcoholics, drug addicts and vagrants; and detention pending deportation or extradition.[343]

III. Requirement of Inform at the Moment of Arrest of the Reasons for that Arrest and any Charges

Article 9 (2) of the ICCPR; Article 5 (2) of the ECHR; and Article 7 (4) of the ACHR provide for this right. The reasons of detention must be given to the detained person immediately.

i. Fox, Campbell and Hartley v The United Kingdom

Bernard Fox and Maire Campbell are husband and wife but separated. Both reside in Belfast, Northern Ireland. On 5 February 1986 they were stopped by the police in Belfast and a full search of the vehicle in which they were travelling was carried out. They were informed that they were being arrested under this section and that this was because the arresting officer suspected them of being terrorists. They were also told that they could be detained for up to 72 hours. After being detained in a police station for approximately 44 hours they were released without any charges being brought against them. Whilst detained, Mr. Fox and Ms Campbell instituted habeas corpus proceedings, but they were released before their applications could be heard by a judge.[344]

Mr. Samuel Hartley, resides in Northern Ireland on 18 August 1986 was arrested at his home. He was informed at the time of his arrest that he was being arrested as he was suspected of being a terrorist. He was taken to Antrim police station where, on arrival, he was shown a copy of the notice of persons held in police custody. [345]

The applicants alleged that they had been victims of Articles 5 (right to liberty of person) and Article 13 (right to a remedy before a national authority in respect of

---

[343] Organization for Security and Co-operation in Europe (OSCE), *Countering Terrorism, Protecting Human Rights: A Manual*, p 152.

[344] *Fox, Campbell and Hartley v. The United Kingdom* [1990] No. 12244/86; 12245/86; 12383/86 (European Court of Human Rights 30 August 1990), paragraph 40 http://www.UNCHR.org/refworld/docid/3ae6b6f90.html [04 March 2013].

[345] *Fox, Campbell and Hartley v. The United Kingdom.*

alleged breaches of the Convention). The case was brought before the ECtHR by the European Commission of Human Rights on 13 July 1989.

In the case of *Fox, Campbell and Hartley v UK*, the ECtHR notes: "This right is an integral part of the scheme of protection afforded by Article 5 of the ECHR." The Court expands this right to all reasons of detention, emphasizing that:

> Article 5 (2) contains the elementary safeguard that any person arrested should know why he is being deprived of his liberty. This provision is an integral part of the scheme of protection afforded by Article 5: by virtue of paragraph 2 any person arrested must be told, in simple, non-technical language that he can understand, the essential legal and factual grounds for his arrest, so as to be able, if he sees fit, to apply to a court to challenge its lawfulness in accordance with art. 5 (4), whilst this information must be conveyed "promptly", it need not be related in its entirety by the arresting officer at the very moment of the arrest. Whether the content and promptness of the information conveyed were sufficient is to be assessed in each case according to its special features.[346]

IV. Obligation to Bring Detainees Promptly before a Judge

Article 9 (3) of the ICCPR; Article 5 (3) of the ECHR; and Article 7 (3) of the ACHR contain provisions requiring detainees to be brought before a judge immediately. For instance Article 9 (3) of the ICCPR provides: "Anyone arrested or detained on a criminal charge shall be brought promptly before a judge or other officer authorized by law to exercise judicial power and shall be entitled to trial within a reasonable time or to release."

i.   Aksoy v. Turkey

Zeki Aksoy, was a Turkish citizen who, lived in Mardin, Kiziltepe, in South-East Turkey, where he was a metalworker. He was born in 1963 and was shot and killed on 16 April 1994. Since then, his father has indicated that he wishes to pursue the case. He was taken into custody on 24 November 1992 at midnight. Approximately twenty policemen had come to his home, and arrested him on suspicion of aiding and abetting PKK terrorists, being a member of the PKK and distributing PKK tracts. On 21 December 1992, the public prosecutor decided that there were no grounds to institute criminal proceedings against the applicant, although eleven of the others

---

[346] *Fox, Campbell and Hartley v. The United Kingdom*, paragraph 40.

detained with him were charged, and no criminal or civil proceedings have been brought in the Turkish courts. The case was referred to the Court on 4 December 1995 by the Government of Turkey and on 12 December 1995 by the European Commission of Human Rights.[347]

The ECtHR, in *Aksoy v Turkey*, held on 18 December 1996 did not accept that detaining persons suspected of terrorism for long periods without judicial intervention was necessary in the fight against terrorism. The Court held:

> It cannot accept that it is necessary to hold a suspect for fourteen days without judicial intervention. This period is exceptionally long, and left the applicant vulnerable not only to arbitrary interference with his right to liberty but also to torture. Moreover, the Government have not adduced any detailed reasons before the Court as to why the fight against terrorism in South-East Turkey rendered judicial intervention impracticable.[348]

The Council of Europe, in the Guideline on Human Rights and Fights against Terrorism, mandates: "A person arrested or detained for terrorist activities shall be brought promptly before a judge. Police custody shall be of a reasonable period of time, the length of which must be provided for by law."[349]

The High Commissioner for Human Rights, in General Comment No 8 concerning the length of detention, stated:

> In certain categories of criminal cases in some countries this matter has caused some concern within the Committee, and members have questioned whether their practices have been in conformity with the entitlement "to trial within a reasonable time or to release" under paragraph 3. Pre-trial detention should be an exception and as short as possible.[350]

V. Provision of the General Rule of the Pre-Trial Detention

---

[347] *Aksoy v. Turkey* [1996] No. 21987/93 (European Court of Human Rights 18 December 1996)   http://hudoc.echr.coe.int/sites/eng/pages/search.aspx?i=001-58003 [06 March 2013]. See, Human Rights Case Digest (1996) VII (3), pp 216-217.

[348] *Aksoy v. Turkey*, paragraph 78.

[349] Council of Europe Guideline on Human Rights and Fights against Terrorism, VII (2).

[350] United Nations High Commissioner for Human Rights, General Comment No. 8 Right to liberty and security of persons, (1982), Sixteenth session, paragraph 3 http://www.unhchr.ch/tbs/doc .nsf/0/f4253f9572cd4700c12563ed00483bec?Opendocument [04 March 2013].

Article 9(3) of the ICCPR; Article 5(3) of the ECHR; and Article 7(5) of the ACHR contain provisions concerning the rules of pre-trial detention. For instance Article 9(3) of the ICCPR states:

> It shall not be the general rule that persons awaiting trial shall be detained in custody, but release may be subject to guarantees to appear for trial, at any other stage of the judicial proceedings, and, should occasion arise, for execution of the judgment.

The period of pre-trial detention strongly depends upon the circumstances in each case. The phrase "reasonable time" included in Article 5(3) of the ECHR depends on the circumstances of a case. It clearly provides that everyone detained person shall be brought promptly before a judge within a reasonable time or to release pending trial.

VI. Right to Take Proceedings before a Court in Order to Determine without Delay the Lawfulness of Detention

The right to challenge the lawfulness of detention (*habeas corpus*) is recognized in Article 9(4) of the ICCPR; Article 5(4) of the ECHR; and Article 7(6) of the ACHR. For instance Article 9(4) of the ICCPR sates:

> 4. Anyone who is deprived of his liberty by arrest or detention shall be entitled to take proceedings before a court, in order that that court may decide without delay on the lawfulness of his detention and order his release if the detention is not lawful.

The Human Rights Commission, in paragraph 16 of General Comment 29, recognized the right of habeas corpus, stating:

> In order to protect non-derogable rights, the right to take proceedings before a court to enable the court to decide without delay on the lawfulness of detention, must not be diminished by a State party's decision to derogate from the Covenant.

i.   Boumediene v. Bush

In 2002 Lakhdar Boumediene and five other Algerian natives were seized by Bosnian police when US intelligence officers suspected their involvement in a plot to attack the US embassy there. The US government classified the men as enemy combatants in the war on terror and detained them at the Guantanamo Bay. Boumediene filed a petition for a writ of habeas corpus, alleging violations of the Constitution's Due Process Clause, various statutes and treaties, the common law, and international law.[351] In *Boumediene v. Bush*, and in contrast to the District Court, the Supreme Court held that the habeas statute extends to non-citizen detainees at Guantanamo, and emphasized "aliens designated as enemy combatants and detained by the US at Guantanamo Bay, are entitled to the right of *habeas corpus*."[352]

The right to proceedings before a court, without delay, concerning the lawfulness of detention depends upon the circumstances of a case. For example, a complex fraud trial that took four years to come to trial; and involved many witnesses and a substantial amount of documentation was not held to violate Article 5 (3). Yet, in a less complex case, delays of over three years did constitute an abused. [353]

VII. Enforceable Right to Compensation for Victims of Unlawful Arrest or Detention

The right to compensation is recognized within a number of international and regional human rights instruments, including Article 9(5) of the ICCPR; Article 5(5) of the ECHR; and Article 10 of the ACHR. The ICCPR within Article 9(5) states: "Anyone who has been the victim of unlawful arrest or detention shall have an enforceable right to compensation."

VIII. Preventive and Indefinite Detentions Following September 11

In regards to counter-terrorism measures and preventive detentions for reasons of public security, the High Commissioner for Human Rights, in General Comment No 8, accepts preventing detentions based on the following specific conditions:

> Also if so-called preventive detention is used, for reasons of public security, it must be controlled by these same provisions, i.e. it must not be arbitrary, and must be based on grounds and procedures established by law (para. 1), information of the reasons must be given (para. 2) and court control of the

---

[351] *Boumediene v. Bush* [2008] No. 06–1195 (United States Court of Appeals for the District of Columbia Circuit 12 June 2008)   http://www.oyez.org/cases/2000-2009/2007/2007_06_1195 [07 March 2013].

[352] *Boumediene v. Bush.*

[353] Organization for Security and Co-operation in Europe (OSCE), *Countering Terrorism, Protecting Human Rights: A Manual*, p 159.

detention must be available (para. 4) as well as compensation in the case of a breach (para. 5). And if, in addition, criminal charges are brought in such cases, the full protection of article 9 (2) and (3), as well as article 14, must also be granted.[354]

After September 11, and following the acceptance of the Armed Conflict model that treats terrorists as combatants, the Bush Administration detained certain individuals based on presidential power provided under Article II of the US Constitution. Furthermore, Section 2 of the A joint Resolution of the White House and the Congress in September 18, 2001 to authorize the use of US Armed Forces against those responsible for the recent attacks launched against the US authorized the use of "all necessary appropriate force". President Bush, The memorandum concerning the Humane Treatment of Taliban and Al-Qaeda Detainees, did not accept that the provisions of Article 3 of the Geneva Conventions were applicable.[355]

i.   Rumsfeld v Padilla

Jose Padilla, an American citizen was arrested upon his return to the US from Pakistan and held as an enemy combatant. Petitioner Padilla was arrested at Chicago's O'Hare Airport upon his return from Pakistan on a material witness warrant. Subsequently, the President issued an order declaring petitioner an enemy combatant. He was held for 18 months without contact with counsel and his family. He appealed for a writ of habeas corpus via a "next friend" Newman.[356]

A plethora of literature exists that criticizes the Bush Administration's preventive detentions approach and their lawfulness in the "war on terror". The Bush Administration stated some reasons to exist of preventive detentions. First, preventive detentions were necessary for interrogation. During litigation concerning Padilla, the Bush Administration conceded that the primary reason for Padilla's detention as an enemy combatant was to find out everything he knew.[357] Second, incapacitation that

---

[354] United Nations High Commissioner for human rights, General Comment No 8, paragraph 4.

[355] Memorandum from President George W. Bush to Vice President Richard (Dick) Cheney, et al. Humane Treatment of Al-Qaeda and Taliban Detainees, 7 February 2002, Paragraph 2 (c), http://www.pegc.us/archive/White_House/bush_memo_20020207_ed.pdf [04 March 2013].

[356] *Ramsfeld v. Padilla et al* [2004] No 03-1027 (Supreme Court of the United States 28 June 2004) https://bulk.resource.org/courts.gov/c/US/542/542.US.426.03-1027.html [04 March 2013].

[357] *Ramsfeld v. Padilla et al.*

could be better applies at the time of armed conflict in the battlefield. Generally, the preventive detentions after September 11 were discriminatory in nature and without any legal framework. With the President Obama Administration, it is time for Congress to enact a comprehensive preventive detention regime to deal with the necessary evil of preventive detention.[358]

Indefinite detention in counter-terrorism measures violates IHRL enshrined within international and regional human rights instruments. For instance, the indefinite detention is incompatible with Article 9 of the ICCPR. Although Article 4 permits temporary derogation from this provision, subject to some conditions only in the public emergency time that threatening the life of the nation.

ii. Belmarsh case

In UK 11 Muslim detainees in the *Belmarsh* prison case, most of whom have been held since December 2001, successfully challenged their indefinite detention and obtained a favourable ruling from the House of Lords on 16 December 2004. The judgment reversed the Court of Appeals finding of October 2002 that indefinite detention was compatible with the UK's human rights obligations and Article 23 of the ATCSA, an act which Lord Bingham and other Lords have ruled to be incompatible with the British Human Rights Act and the ECHR.[359] In particular, the Lords found that indefinite detention discriminates on the grounds of nationality (Article 14 of the ECHR) because it applies only to foreign nationals suspected of terrorism, notwithstanding a comparable threat from terrorist suspects holding UK nationality. Persons suspected of terrorism in the US have been similarly subjected to indefinite detention.[360]

iii. Hamdi v. Rumsfeld

---

[358] S. Cooper Blum 'Why and How of Preventive Detention in the War on Terror' (2009) 26 (1) *Thomas M. Cooley Law Review*, pp52, 59, 76, and 111.

[359] *A (FC) and others (FC) v. Secretary of State for the Home Department* [2004] UKHL 71 (House of Lords Appellate Committee 16 December 2004), paragraph 231 http://www.publications.parliament.uk/pa/ld200405/ldjudgmt/jd041216/a&oth-1.htm [04 March 2013].

[360] A. de Zayas, 'Human rights and indefinite detention' (2005) 87 (857) *International Review of the Red Cross*, pp 23-25.

Since January 2002, more than 700 persons have been held as terrorism suspects at the naval base in Guantanamo Bay, following the Military Order of President Bush. On 28 June 2004, the US Supreme Court rejected the fiction of the existence of a legal black hole and held that the persons being held in Guantanamo Bay are entitled to counsel and to challenge the legality of their detention. American citizens have been held incommunicado alongside foreign nationals and subjected to indefinite detention as "enemy combatants." One of them, Yaser Hamdi, was initially held in Guantanamo and subsequently transferred to a naval brig in Charleston, South Carolina, where he was held in solitary confinement. In the case of *Hamdi v. Rumsfeld*, the US Supreme Court upheld the government's right to hold US citizens as enemy combatants without criminal charges when they had been seized on the battlefield participating in active hostilities, but noted that "no citizen shall be imprisoned or otherwise detained by the US except pursuant to an Act of Congress."[361]

Both municipal and international law provide justifiable rights to persons deprived of detention. The policy makers must pose and answer the following question: "Is that of the legitimate objectives of detention?" If the purpose is national security, a balancing of rights must take place.[362]

iv.   Moriana Hernandez Valentini de Bazzano v. Uruguay

Luis Maria Bazzano Ambrosini, was detained on 3 April 1975 and immediately thereafter subjected to various forms of tortured such as forced to remain standing for 14 hours, electric shocks and bastinado (blows). He was accused of complicity in "assistance to subversive association" for having participated in a spontaneous demonstration and was placed at the disposal of a military judge, although the accusation was consistently denied by the prisoner.[363] The Inter-American Human Rights Commission, in the *Maria Bazzano* decision, declared that the detention

---

[361] *Yaser Esam Hamdi et al v. Rumsfeld* [2004] No. 03-6696 (United States Supreme Court 28 June 2004) http://caselaw.lp.findlaw.com/scripts/getcase.pl?court=us&vol=000&invol=03-6696 [04 March 2013].

[362] A. Zayas, 'Human rights and indefinite detention', *International Review of the Red Cross*, pp 36-37.

[363] *Moriana Hernandez Valentini de Bazzano v. Uruguay* [1979] No. 5/1977 UN.Doc. CCPR/C/OP/1 (Inter-American Human Rights Commission 18 April 1977), paragraph 2 http://www1.umn.edu/humanrts/undocs/html/5_1977b.htm [04 March 2013].

constituted a violation of Article 9 (1) of the ICCPR on the basis that "he remained in custody despite a judicial order for his release." [364]

State counter-terrorism measures have an impact on the liberty of persons, including pre-trial procedures for terrorist offences. As a part of counter-terrorism measures, States may lawfully detain terrorism suspects, however any such measures must at least provide for judicial scrutiny and the ability of detained persons to have the lawfulness of their detention determined by a judicial authority. The observance of due process and the right to a fair trial is important and serves as a safeguard for the liberty and security of persons.[365]

5.1.5   The Right to Privacy

Lord Lester defines privacy as "the presumption that individuals should have an area of autonomous development, interaction and liberty, a "private sphere" with or without interaction with others and free from state intervention and free from excessive unsolicited intervention by other uninvited individuals."[366] The right to privacy is not a non-derogable right, and could be limited by observation of the specific conditions. This right is discussed under the issues related to private life of individuals and information about the person's identity

a) The Right to Privacy within International Instruments

The right to privacy is enshrined and protected through a number of international and regional human rights treaties. Article 12 of UDHR provides: "No one shall be subjected to arbitrary interference with his privacy, family, home or correspondence, nor to attacks upon his honour and reputation. Everyone has the right to the protection of the law against such interference or attacks."

Article 17 (1) of the ICCPR; Article 11 (2) of the ACHR; and Article 8 (1) ECHR address the right in virtually identical terms. Article 17 (1) of the ICCPR

---

[364] *Moriana Hernandez Valentini de Bazzano v. Uruguay*, paragraph 10.
[365] Office of the United Nations High Commissioner for Human Rights (OHCHR), 'Human Rights, Terrorism and Counter-Terrorism, Factsheet, No 32, pp 36-37.
[366] Lord Lester of Herne Hill, and David Pannick (Eds.), *Human Rights Law & Practice*, second edition, 2004, Butterworth, London, paragraph 4, 82.

provides: "No one shall be subjected to arbitrary or unlawful interference with his privacy, family, home or correspondence, nor to unlawful attacks on his honour and reputation."

The High Commissioner for Human Rights, in paragraph 6 of the General Comment No 16 on the right to respect of privacy, family, home and correspondence, and protection of honour and reputation, prohibits the violation against this right. It provides:

> Article 17 affords protection to personal honour and reputation and States are under an obligation to provide adequate legislation to that end. Provision must also be made for everyone effectively to be able to protect himself against any unlawful attacks that do occur and to have an effective remedy against those responsible.

b) **Requirement of the Legality**

Any act which affects the person's privacy must be lawfully conducted and must be prescribed by law. Additionally, such legislation must not be unjust, unpredictable or unreasonable. In addition, the law must specify the circumstances of the permitted interferences in a non-discriminatory manner and the law must contain with the obligations of arbitrary exercise of interfering privacy.[367]

The right to privacy is not a non-derogable right. However, any limitation on this right of the legal authority should take place on the basis of law. The High Commissioner for Human Rights, in paragraph 3 of the General Comment No 16, states:

> The term "unlawful" means that no interference can take place except in cases envisaged by the law. Interference authorized by States can only take place on the basis of law, which itself must comply with the provisions, aims and objectives of the Covenant.

The ECHR establishes conditions for any interference with the right in Article 8(2), as follows:

---

[367] Office of the United Nations High Commissioner for Human Rights (OHCHR), 'Human Rights, Terrorism and Counter-Terrorism, Factsheet, No 32, p 45.

There shall be no interference by a public authority with the exercise of this right except such as is in accordance with the law and is necessary in a democratic society in the interests of national security, public safety or the economic well-being of the country, for the prevention of disorder or crime, for the protection of health or morals, or for the protection of the rights and freedoms of others.

I. *Klass and others v Federal Republic of Germany*

Klass and others v Federal Republic of Germany was based upon the arrest of a woman on suspicion of drunken driving. The applicant alleged that she was beaten up and seriously injured by two policemen in the presence of her eight year old daughter. The existence of injuries was confirmed by subsequent medical examinations. She filed criminal charges and the Head of the Detmold District Administration dismissed her complaints concerning the officers on the ground that the use of force had been justified and not disproportionate. The case was referred to the ECtHR based on the violation against Article 8 of the ECHR. Mrs. Klass complained that as the aforementioned treatment took place on private property in the presence of her eight year-old daughter, it had also given rise to a breach of her right to respect for her private and family life under Article 8. On 6 September 1978, the ECtHR decided that:

> Since the facts on which Mrs Klass relied were not established, her daughter's complaints were likewise unfounded. The activity or danger against which a particular series of surveillance measures is directed may continue for years, even decades, after the suspension of those measures. Subsequent notification to each individual affected by a suspended measure might well jeopardize the long-term purpose that originally prompted the surveillance. [368]

The right to privacy can be affected by electronic surveillance and data processing, both of which are considered essential weapons in the fight against international terrorism. Computer-based monitoring techniques, indicating patterns of communication, can be used to direct surveillance programs in geographical areas and identify individual targets.[369]

---

[368] *Klass and others v. Federal Republic of Germany* [1979] Series A, No28 (European Court of Human Rights 6 September 1979), paragraph 57, http://hudoc.echr.coe.int/sites/eng/pages/search.as px?i=001-57510 [04 March 2013].

[369] I. Cameron, 'General Human Rights Principles Relevant to US-EU Counter-terrorism Cooperation', in C. Fijnaut et al, *Legal Instruments in the Fight against International Terrorism,: A Transatlantic Dialogue*, 2004, Brill Academic Publishers, pp 357-358.

In regards to the collection and processing of personal data, the Council of Europe Guidelines on Human Rights and Fight against Terrorism states that processing personal data may lead to interference with rights to privacy by the relevant authorities. The Guidelines elaborate upon the issue as follows:

> Within the context of the fight against terrorism, the collection and the processing of personal data by any competent authority in the field of State security may interfere with the respect for private life only if such collection and processing, in particular: (i) are governed by appropriate provisions of domestic law; (ii) are proportionate to the aim for which the collection and the processing were foreseen; (iii) may be subject to supervision by an external independent authority.[370]

II. Malone v. UK

The ECtHR, in _Malone v. UK_, examined issues concerning the right to private life and correspondence. James Malone was an antique dealer charged with a number of offences relating to the dishonest handling of stolen goods in 1977. At the first trial, details of a telephone conversation of Malone were contained in the note-book of the police officer in charge of the investigations. Counsel for the prosecution accepted that this conversation had been intercepted on the authority of a warrant issued by the Secretary of State for the Home Department. Malone believed that both his correspondence and his telephone calls had been intercepted for a number of years and had been "metered" on behalf of the police by a device that automatically records all numbers dialled. On September 1978, the applicant requested the Post Office and the complaints department of the police to remove suspected listening devices from his telephone. Both the Post Office and the police replied that they had no authority in the matter. The Courts held that the interception of communications occurred on behalf of the police for the purposes of the prevention and detection of crime. The case was referred to the Court by the European Commission of Human Rights on 16 May 1983 based upon the potential violation of Article 8 of the ECHR. The ECtHR held that:

> The law must be sufficiently clear in its terms to give citizens an adequate indication as to the circumstances in which and the conditions on which public

---

[370] Council of Europe Guidelines on Human Rights and Fight against Terrorism, V.

authorities are empowered to resort to this secret and potentially dangerous interference with the right to respect for private life and correspondence.[371]

c) **Requirement of Proportionality and Necessity**

The Council of Europe Guideline on Human Rights and Fight against Terrorism states that counter-terrorism measures which may interfere with the right to privacy must be provided for by law and the lawfulness of such actions able to be challenged in court.[372] In addition, the Guideline adds that any counter measures must be based upon proportionality and necessity. It provides:

> Measures taken to fight terrorism must be planned and controlled by the authorities so as to minimise, to the greatest extent possible, recourse to lethal force and, within this framework, the use of arms by the security forces must be strictly proportionate to the aim of protecting persons against unlawful violence or to the necessity of carrying out a lawful arrest.[373]

In regards to US counter-terrorism measures, anyone suspected to be involved in international terrorism through aiding, abetting, financing or harbouring terrorism is now subject to far greater government intrusions into the privacy of homes and offices. For example, according to Section 212 of the PATRIOT Act, telephone and e-mail communications, and such personal practices as checking out books from libraries or purchasing them from bookstores. However, these practices might be occurred in good faith, necessary, and reasonability without excess.[374]

Following the September 11, President Bush acknowledged that he had ordered the National Security Agency to conduct an electronic eavesdropping program in the US without first obtaining warrants, and said he would continue the highly classified program because it was a vital tool in our war against the terrorists. Bush defended his action as fully consistent with my constitutional responsibilities and authorities.[375] The Presidential order to conduct an electronic eavesdropping

---

[371] *Malone v. The United Kingdom* [1984] No. 8691/79 (European Court of Human Rights 2 August 1984), paragraph 67 http://hudoc.echr.coe.int/sites/eng/pages/search.aspx?i=001-57533 [05 March 2013].

[372] Council of Europe Guidelines on Human Rights and Fight against Terrorism, XIV.

[373] Council of Europe Guideline on Human Rights and Fight against Terrorism, VI.

[374] D. Cassel, 'International Human Rights and the United States Response to 11 September', pp 293-294.

[375] D. E. Sanger, 'Bush Says He Ordered Domestic Spying', The New York Times, 18 December 2005 http://www.nytimes.com/2005/12/18/politics/18bush.html?adxnnl=1&adxnnlx

program is considered as gross violation against the right to privacy of individuals supported by various international and regional human rights instruments.

Any effective counter-terrorism measure is likely to interfere with privacy rights. It is, therefore, important to understand the extent to which it is lawful to interfere with these rights. Law enforcement agencies have at their disposal a comprehensive array of tools and procedures that can be used in counter-terrorism operations. These range from traditional policing methods, such as carrying out a physical search of a suspect, to the use of highly sophisticated eavesdropping surveillance equipment. All of these will interfere, to varying degrees, with rights to privacy. To be lawful, they must be justified as prescribed by law; necessary in a democratic society; and proportionate.[376]

In general, States have a clear obligation and duty to protect the safety and well-being of their citizens, while at the same time protecting the rule of law, fundamental rights and genuine democratic orders. A balance between these two interests is often difficult to achieve. From a legal point of view, this situation can create significant challenges. The State must ensure its action is reasonable in order to fulfil its duties, but it should prevent creating a system of governance that risks breaking down the pillars of a democratic society under the guise of combating terrorism.[377]

5.2 CONCLUSION

The relation between human rights and terrorism is found in both the rights of the terrorist victims and the perpetrators of terrorist acts. The human rights issues that emerge from the counter-terrorism terrorism range from the abuse of the right to life and right to security of terrorist victims to the violation of the perpetrators' right to a fair trial; and prohibitions against arbitrary detention and torture.

=1134932474-1PowQ0+hICaF804jJDegmQ&_r=0 [08 March 2013].

[376] Organization for Security and Co-operation in Europe (OSCE), *Countering Terrorism, Protecting Human Rights: A Manual*, pp 200-201.

[377] B. Bekink, 'A Dilemma of the Twenty-first Century State: Questions on the Balance between Democracy and Security' (2005) 5 (2) *African Human Rights Law Journal*, pp 421-423.

Following the attacks of September 11, human rights values, which have been painstakingly crafted over a period of decades, were scarified in the absence of any legal standard and framework for the States counter-measures. Aspects of the counter-terrorism measures adopted by States led to the undermining protections accorded under IHRL following the enactment of draconian anti-terrorism legislation and increased security measures, such as the abuse of the right to fair trial for accused persons. In some cases, the fight against terrorism was considered an opportunity for authoritarian regimes to repress opposition groups and restrict fundamental freedoms under the guise of counter-terrorism measures.

It is wrong to conclude that increasing the civil liberties may be enlarging the risk of terrorist attacks in societies. In fact preferences of security measures than fundamental liberties, which have been supported by international and regional human rights instruments, compose an insecurity atmosphere in society that is suitable for any terrorist activities. The protection of the individual rights against security measures is a result of good government that is completely consistent with IHRL.

Counter-terrorism measures perspectives, such as law enforcement approach or military approach, should apply human rights as legal standards and framework to prevent violation against the rights of individuals. The present chapter focused on specific instrumental human rights provisions that are protected by the majority of the international human rights instruments that are undermined as a result of counter-terrorism measures, including:

i.   The right to life by focusing on the death penalty and extrajudicial executions in counter-terrorism process;

ii. Right to freedom from torture and cruel, inhuman or degrading treatment or punishment by focusing on the prohibition of torture and cruel inhumane treatment;

iii. The right to fair trial by focusing on the principle of legality, equality before the law, the right to presumption innocence, right to hear from a competent authority, right to call witnesses, right to appeal;

iv. The right to liberty and security by focusing on the prohibition of indefinite detentions, and prohibition of arbitrary arrest;

v. The right to privacy by focusing on the private life and security of correspondence.

In conclusion the IHRL should be recognized as the international legal framework in all counter-terrorism measures including the law enforcement measures and military force measures. Opposing against the applicability of IHRL based on the reason that the "war against terrorism" is an armed conflict, therefore the IHL considers as the only applicable law in the time of armed conflicts is not legal and logical analysis. Thus, as frequently emphasized by the UN and its bodies the IHRL is not only the law of the peace time, but it is the rights to maximize protection of human beings in both situations of war and peace. Moreover, the present chapter concludes that the rule of law and respect for human rights are considered the essential factors to achieving a balance between the maintenance of the security and respect for human rights in counter-terrorism processes.

CHAPTER VI

CONCLUSION

INTRODUCTION

Undoubtedly, terrorism is considered a significant threat by States authorities. Terrorism, due to its destructive effect on the social structures of States, propels governments to confront the danger of terrorism. Nowadays, the necessity of counter-terrorism measures inside the borders of States to fight against domestic-terrorism is not avoidable. While States have a duty to protect civilians against terrorist acts through the use of effective counter-terrorism policies to save lives, the establishment of a legal framework for counter-terrorism measures is the duty of States as well. When counter terrorism measures are adopted by governments, the rule of law should serve as a guideline. The power of governments is not unlimited in counter-terrorism policies and it must be limited based upon national laws and regulations; and international legal norms.

Terrorism is no longer considered a domestic threat. Despite the international nature of terrorist attacks, which can be financially supported thousand miles far from the operation centre, the negative effects of terrorism on the global economy and the security of international society is pervasive. For example, the September 11 attacks in the US led to a multi-national war in the Middle East. The September 11 attacks in the US led to significant changes in the political systems of the States of Afghanistan and Iraq. The violations of international law, specifically IHRL and IHL, committed through the adoption of wrongful counter-terrorism policies and measures have resulted in thousands of fatalities; billions of dollars in economic damages; and perpetual global insecurity.

The proliferation of terror attacks in recent years illustrates the inability of State counter-terrorism measures and efforts of the international community to determine and remedy the roots and causes of terrorism. The deadlock in efforts to reach consensus on a universally accepted definition of terrorism is demonstrative of the aforementioned assertion. It is obvious that the apparent ignorance regarding the terrorist phenomenon leads to the adoption of wrongful and illegal counter-terrorism measures, particularly on the part of States that have been victims of terrorist acts.

6.1.1   History

Studying the history of terrorism is valuable in recognizing the acts, actors, methods and behaviour of terrorists during the time of their emergence and evolution. The history of terrorism shows how societies have fought against this type of violence and how terrorism has been used in struggles against autocratic governors. The study of the historical evolution of terrorism helps to distinguish terrorism from other forms of existing violence.

The review of the history of terrorism is not simply a glance at historical acts because it illustrates the tactics and the motives behind the use of violence by terrorists throughout history. In fact, the historical review of terrorism within this thesis studies the structure of terrorism. For instance, the study of terrorism in the contemporary era highlights the structural differences between 'modern terrorism' and 'ancient terrorism'. The first approach taken regarding the history of terrorism in the present thesis explains the methods, tactics and behaviours of terrorism phenomenon in history to help identify the changes that distinguish terrorism from other forms of violence, such as crime and war. Additionally, the review also partially explores how terrorism has involved over the centuries and how the tactics have evolved with the passage of time.

The first historical period examined within the present research is the Ancient Time. During this period, the existence of terrorism in the Assyrian and the Roman empires is reviewed. Based upon the study of the issue by historians, terrorism was common and, in some cases, considered as a civil duty to attack tyrants during this period.

The review of the history of terrorism in the "Middle Ages" and the "Early Modern Era" examines terrorism in the context of both Western and Eastern histories. The use of tyrannicide as a justification for violence in the Church and the State conflict in Europe and the political assassinations by the Assassins in Iran during the "Middle Ages" are surveyed. In the early modern era, the French revolution, which is considered State terrorism, and the beginning of the developments of the notion of terrorism are analyzed. Anarchists and terrorist activities in Europe; the effect of terrorist groups in the beginning of World War I; the use of guerrilla warfare in Spain, Russia and other parts of the globe; and the use of terror to obtain independence are other issues discussed regarding the history of terrorism in the early modern era.

6.1.2   Counter-Terrorism and Human Rights Violations

Counter-terrorism measures pursued as protective measures for human beings against destructive acts of terrorists can negatively affect the rights of the person the measures are intended to protect. Any failure in the duty of officials engaged in counter-terrorism activities can violate human rights that are protected through various international and regional human rights instruments.

A number of the State counter-terrorism measures pursued under the guise of security contradict human rights norms. It is correct that terrorism, by its very nature, is a serious threat to the rights of individuals, such as right to life and right to liberty and security of persons. However, the effects of the adoption of wrongful counter-terrorism measures on human rights are no less detrimental than the negative effects of terrorism on human rights. Thus, as one of the main issues of current thesis, Chapter V focuses on some of the fundamental human rights that are jeopardized by State counter-terrorism measures employed in both the law enforcement and military force approach to counter-terrorism measures.

a)   Recognition of Human Rights

Human rights belong to all people of the globe and have three specific characteristics: they are equal, inalienable and universal rights. International human rights are divided into three generations by Vasak: civil and political rights; economic, social, and cultural rights; and solidarity rights.

Human rights are flexible rights, which mean that they may be limited or suspended under certain circumstances. Contemporary debates typically focus on the "limitation" and "derogation" of human rights. In regards to the limitation of human rights, permission for State limitation of human rights exists in some human rights instruments, but three essential conditions exist for the imposition of a limitation: prescribed by law; pursuant to a legitimate purpose; and arising from a condition of necessity and proportionality. Thus, any limitation should be applied based on the observation of three aforementioned conditions. However, the derogation of specific human rights is only possible in the special circumstances, such as a time of public emergency or war.

b) The Link between Human Rights and Counter-Terrorism

Human rights and counter-terrorism are linked together with the rights of terrorist actors and the rights of the victims of terrorist acts. The IHL supervises on the observation of the rights of both groups. It protects the rights of the victims of terrorist acts and at the same time supervises the rights of terrorist suspects to prevent any violation against their fundamental human rights during the detention, and trial.

The UN emphasizes the protection of human rights while pursuing counter-terrorism measures. The activities of UN bodies in this regard are extensively reviewed. Through this review, the statements of the Secretary General and the Human Rights Commission; and resolutions adopted by the SC and GA concerning the protection of human rights while pursuing counter-terrorism measures; and the GA and SC Resolutions are examined. Due to the emphasis placed on the protection of human rights while countering terrorism by the UN, the conclusion was reached that the declaration by the US of a "war on terrorism" has seriously challenged human rights values following the September 11 attacks because it was a war declared against a non-State terrorist group harboured in another State's territory. As a result of this war, human rights have been widely restricted, violated, and ignored.

c) Counter-Terrorism Negative Impacts on Certain Human Rights

The destructive effects of wrongful counter-terrorism measures on some certain human rights are explored in Chapter V and include the right to life; the right to fair trial; the right to liberty and security; and the right to privacy. The rights that are more prone to violate by counter-terrorism measures are recognized and analyzed together with the related case law. All of the discussed rights are reviewed through the examination of the relevant provisions enshrined within international human rights instruments to determine the legal sources of the discussed rights.

I. Violation against the Right to Life

The use of the lethal force; the existence of the death penalty; and the targeted killings of suspected terrorist are three serious challenges that threaten the life of persons. Based upon human rights norms enshrined within international instruments, counter-terrorism agents are not free to use of force except in necessary and unavoidable situations; and to the extent required for the performance of their duty. The United Nations Basic Principles on the Use of Force and Firearms by Law Enforcement Officials provides the relevant legal framework. In relation to the right to life, the cases of *Tennessee v Garner*; *Neira Alegria v Peru*; *McKerr v United Kingdom*; *McCann and Others v. United Kingdom*; *Ergi v Turkey*; and *Jean Charles de Menezes* were reviewed. Finally, through the review of international and regional instruments and case law, the conclusion reached is that the use of force is not an unlimited power available to law enforcement officials when engaged in counter-terrorism measures. The use of force is limited based upon specific circumstances relating to proportionality; necessity; and the extent such force is required for the performance of their duty.

In addition, the issue of the prohibition against the death penalty within human rights instruments is examined. The existence of the death penalty as a punishment for terrorist crimes; the potential imposition of such a penalty in special tribunals, such as the US military commissions; and the case law of the *US v Khalid Sheikh Mohammed* illustrate the risks of violations of the right to life during counter-terrorism measures.

The subject of targeted killing is one of the main concerns in the Human Rights Commission and the Special Rapporteurs communications, which condemn the use of a drone to attack alleged terrorists in the US. Consideration of the US responds to the Special Rapporteurs communications led to the applicability of IHRL and the competence of the Human Rights Commission in armed conflicts. In this regard, the ICJ, PACE, and the ICRC positions are examined, which confirm the positions of Special Rapporteurs concerning the applicability of the IHRL provisions in the situation of armed conflicts alongside the provisions of the IHL. Despite the disparities, the conclusion reached was that IHRL is not merely the applicable law in peace time or in domestic law enforcement response to terrorism, but is a series of protective norms that are enacted to act as an umbrella framework to protect the rights of innocent people during times of peace and times of armed conflicts. Therefore, IHL and IHRL are complementary, not mutually exclusive. The prime target of the IHRL enactment is the creation of a protective framework for human beings against any abuse of their rights, therefore expanding the competence of the applicability of human rights is accordance with the prime target of the IHRL enactment, and applying of any limitation against it harms the rights of individuals and is in the contrast with the main target of the IHRL.

II. Violation against the Right to Freedom from Torture and Cruel, Inhuman or Degrading Treatment or Punishment

These issues were examined according to international and regional human rights instruments; and case law, which included *Chahal v United Kingdom*; and *Selcuk and Asker v Turkey*. Through the review of the instruments and case law, the conclusion reached is that this right is vastly protected within both IHRL and IHL provisions; and the use of any types of torture, cruel, inhuman and degrading punishment and treatment during counter-terrorism measures is absolutely prohibited.

III. Violation against the Right to Fair Trial

The right to fair trial is first examined based on protective international and regional instrumental provisions. This right is extensively discussed together with other basic related rights of the persons in a trial, such as the principle of legality; equality before the law or equal treatment by the law; the right to presumption of innocence; the right to a hearing with due guarantees and within a reasonable time by a competent, independent and impartial tribunal; the right to call witnesses; the right to legal assistance; the right to be informed promptly in understandable language; the right to adequate time for the preparation of defence and the right to access to evidence and documents; and the right to appeal to a higher tribunal. Alongside the discussions on the violation of the aforementioned rights during counter-terrorism measures, the cases of *Ecer and Zeyrek v Turkey*; *Heaney and McGuinness v Ireland*; *Castillo Petruzzi v. Peru*; *Doorson v The Netherlands* are analyzed. Generally, right to fair trial is one of the most extensive human rights and contains of a series of important rights of individuals in a trial. Despite the fact that this right is not absolute and can be restricted in special circumstances, respect for this right, especially in relation to terrorism, is vital because of the nature of terrorist crimes and the seriousness of the punishments for such offenses, which include capital punishment or life imprisonment.

IV. Violation against the Right to Liberty and Security

Ensuring the right to liberty and security of individuals is the duty of governments. However, striking a balance between the security and liberty of individuals can guarantee the observation of the right. The right is protected by international and regional human rights instruments; and discussed under other basic rights, including prohibition against arbitrary arrest and detention; the requirement of establishment by law of any deprivation of liberty; the requirement to be informed at the moment of arrest of the reasons for that arrest and any charges; the obligation to bring detainees promptly before a judge; the provision of the general rule of the pre-trial detention; the right to take proceedings before a court in order to determine, without delay, the lawfulness of detention; the enforceable right to compensation for victims of unlawful arrest or detention; and the prohibition against preventive and indefinite detentions. During the discussions on the violation of this right, some of the related case law examined includes *Fox, Campbell and Hartley v UK*; *Aksoy v Turkey*; *Boumediene v. Bush*; *Padilla v Rumsfeld*; *Belmarsh* case; *Hamdi v. Rumsfeld*; and *Moriana Hernandez Valentini de Bazzano v. Uruguay*.

Generally, the right to liberty and security of persons can be easily violated by States during counter-terrorism measures. To protect society, States may lawfully detain terrorism suspects. However, any such measures must be based on the respect for the liberty of persons. Here, striking a balance between the respect for human rights and the security of States can balance the scale of justice.

V. Violation against the Right to Privacy

The right of individuals to privacy is a derogable right, which is supported by a number of international and regional instruments. However, the observation of special circumstances, which include the requirement of legality, necessity and proportionality for any limitation, is required. *Klass and others v Federal Republic of Germany*; and *Malone v. UK* are two cases that illustrate the need to respect the right to privacy in counter-terrorism and the requirement of legality within the court decisions. Following the September 11 attacks, the right to privacy has been widely violated by States under the pretext of security. For example, in the US, the surveillance of correspondence occurred by Presidential order and the PATRIOT Act permits surveillance of civilian communications as a justified counter-terrorism measure within Section 212.

6.2 FINDINGS

International law obliges States to dynamically prevent and combat terrorism; and prohibits any State support of terrorism, which is reflected in various UN Resolutions (e.g., SC Resolution 1373). However, the existence of such international legal obligations is not sufficient. The increased emphasis within the international community of States to combat terrorism, especially following the September 11 attacks, has become an extraordinary opportunity for some States to restrict the fundamental rights of individuals under the guise of counter-terrorism measures.

Following the September 11 attacks, the military approach of counter-terrorism replaced the law enforcement counter-terrorism approach of the States. Preferring the militaristic response instead of the law enforcement response by States imposed serious threats to the right of civilians in the armed conflict under the pretext of war against terrorism.

Through the review of terrorism in different historical epochs, the present study finds that the history of human civilization is plagued by episodes of violence. The image of terrorism, as one of the main origin of violence, differs throughout history. For instance, terrorism during the "Middle Ages" was considered as an act against tyranny, however the image changed following the widespread use of terrorism by regimes against political oppositions as a tool of suppression. At the end of the previous century, the image of terrorism consisted of bomb-throwing by anarchist groups in order to reach political targets. Today, the popular image of terrorism focuses upon transnational extremist Islamist groups. Hence, reviewing the history of terrorism illustrates diverse types of terrorism and evolutions in terrorism.

The review of the counter-terrorism measures demonstrates the importance of these protective measures. Undoubtedly, society must be secure against the threats of terrorists. At first glance, counter-terrorism measures can be considered defensive measures that protect the rights of individuals against any violation by terrorism, including the right to life and the right to security. However, the extensive use of counter-terrorism can negatively affect the rights of civilians as well. States, for example, under the guise of counter-terrorism measures, can restrict civil liberties. Moreover, counter-terrorism measures can be used to abrogate the rights of accused terrorists or political opponents who are labelled "terrorists", as has shown in numerous precedents. Concerns about the violation of human rights under the cover of counter-terrorism reached an apex following the September 11 attacks and the declaration of "war against terrorism" by the US.

BIBLIOGRAPHY

1. A. B. Krueger et al, 'Education, Poverty, Political Violence and Terrorism: Is There a Casual Connection?' (2002) No. w9074 *National Bureau of Economic Research Cambridge*.
2. A. Cassese, 'Terrorism is also Disrupting Some Crucial Legal Categories of International Law' (2001) 12(5) *European Journal of International law (EJIL)*.
3. A. Conte, *Hand Book on Human Rights Compliance While Countering Terrorism*, Centre on Global Counter-Terrorism Cooperation, 2008, 13 http://www.globalct.org/images/content /pdf/reports/human_rights_handbook.pdf
4. A. D. Amato, 'Human Rights as Part of Customary International Law: A Plea for Change of Paradigms', (2010), *Northwestern University School of Law Scholarly Common*, Faculty Working Papers, Paper 88. http://scholarlycommons.law.northwestern.edu/facultyworkingpa pers/88
5. A. de Zayas, 'Human rights and indefinite detention' (2005) 87 (857) *International Review of the Red Cross*.
6. A. H. Garrison, 'How the World Changed: A History of the Development of Terrorism', *Criminal Justice Planning Coordinator Delaware Criminal Justice Council*.
7. A. J. Langlois, 'Human Rights', in R. Devetak et al, *An Introduction to International Relations: Australian Perspectives*, Cambridge University Press, New York, 2008.
8. A. Maskaliunaite, 'Defining Terrorism in the Political and Academic Discourses' (2002) 2 (8) *Baltic Defence Review*.
9. A. P. Schmid, 'Terrorism-The Definitional Problem' (2004) 36 (2) and (3) *Case Western Reserve Journal of International Law*.
10. A. Zwitter, *Human Security, Law and the Prevention of Terrorism*, Routledge, New York, 2011.
11. A.G. Hamid, 'Islamic International Law and the Rights of Self-Defence of State' (2009) 2 (1) *Journal of East Asia and International Law*.
12. Amnesty International, 'Torture in the Eighties' (1973) http://www.ucl.ac.uk/clinical-psychology/Research-Groups/PainSIG/definitions.htm
13. A. Williams et al, *Terror Attacks*, Futura, London, 2006.
14. B. Bekink, 'A Dilemma of the Twenty-first Century State: Questions on the Balance between Democracy and Security' (2005) 5 (2) *African Human Rights Law Journal*.
15. B. Ganor, 'Defining Terrorism: Is One Man's Terrorist Another Man's Freedom Fighter?' (2002), 3 (4), *Police Practice and Research*.
16. B. Spalek, Introducing Counter-Terrorism studies, in B. Spalek (ed.), *Counter-Terrorism: Community Base Approaches to Preventing Terror Crime*, Palgrave Macmillan, London, 2012.
17. B.S. Lawrence, 'Historical Perspective: Using the Past to Study the Present' (1984) 9 (2), *The Academy of Management Review*.
18. Bloomberg Law, Case briefs of Tennessee v. Garner http://www.casebriefs.com/blog/law/criminal-law/criminal-law-keyed-to-lafave/justification-and-excuse/tennessee-v-garner-4/]

19. C. B. Muelle et al, *Evidence: Practice under Rules*, New York, Wolters Kluwer, 1999.
20. C. Lumina, 'Counter Terrorism Legislation and the Protection of Human Rights: A survey of Selected International Practice' (2007) 7 (1) *African Human Rights Law Journal*.
21. C. Tomuschat, 'Human Rights and International Humanitarian Law' (2010) 21 (1) *The European Journal of International Law (EJIL)*.
22. D. A. Mundis, 'The Use of Military Commissions to Prosecute Individuals Accused of Terrorist Acts' (2002) 96 (2) *The American Journal of International Law*.
23. D. Cassel, 'International Human Rights and the United States Response to 11 September', in C. Fijnaut et al, *Legal Instruments in the Fight against International Terrorism: A Transatlantic Dialogue*, 2004, Brill Academic Publishers.
24. D. E. Sanger, 'Bush Says He Ordered Domestic Spying', The New York Times, 18 December 2005 http://www.nytimes.com/2005/12/18/politics/18bush.html?adxnnl=1&adxnnlx=11 34932474-1PowQ0+hICaF804jJDegmQ&_r=0
25. D. F. Vagts, 'Which Court Should Try Persons Accused of Terrorism' (2003) 14 (2) *European Journal of International Law (EJIL)*.
26. D. G. Evans, 'Human Rights: Four Generations Practice and Development', in A. Abdi et al (eds), *Education for Human Rights and Global Citizenship*, Albany: SUNY Press, 2008.
27. D. Kretzmer, 'Targeted Killing of Suspected Terrorists: Extra-Judicial Executions or Legitimate Means of Defence?' (2005) 16 (2) *The European Journal of International Law (EJIL)*.
28. D. Marty. 2007. Second Report of the Committee on Legal Affairs and Human Rights. *Parliamentary Assembly of the Council of Europe (PACE)*. Report on Secret detentions and illegal transfers of detainees involving Council of Europe Member States. Strasbourg: Council of Europe.
29. D. Write-Neville, Global Terrorism, in R. Devetak et al (ed.), *An Introduction to International Relations, Australian Perspectives*, Cambridge University Press, New York, 2007.
30. Death Penalty Information Centre (DPIC), 'U.S. to Seek Death Penalty under New Military Commissions' http://www.deathpenaltyinfo.org/us-seek-death-penalty-under-new-military-commiss ions
31. E. F. Reid et al, Domain Mapping of Contemporary Terrorism Research, in H. Chen (eds.) *et al, Terrorism Informatics: Knowledge Management and Data Mining for Homeland Security*, Springer, New York, 2008.
32. E. F. Reid, et al, 'Mapping the Contemporary Terrorism Research Domain' (2007) 65 (1) *International Journal of Human-Computer Studies*.
33. E. Stubbins Batesand et al, *Terrorism and International Law, Accountability, Remedies, and Reforms*, 2011, Oxford University Press, New York.
34. E. Stubbins Batesand et al, *Terrorism and International Law, Accountability, Remedies, and Reforms*, 2011, Oxford University Press, New York.
35. E. Stubbins Batesand et al, *Terrorism and International Law, Accountability, Remedies, and Reforms*, 2011, Oxford University Press, New York.
36. F. Daftary, 'Introduction to The Assassins Legends: Myth of the Ismailis' (1994) *The Institute of Ismaili Studies*.

37. G. Chaliand et al, *The history of terrorism: from antiquity to al Qaeda*, University of California Press, Berkeley, 2007.
38. G. Martin, *Essentials of Terrorism: Concepts and Controversies*, Sage, California, 2011.
39. G. Martin, *Essentials of Terrorism: Concepts and Controversies*, Sage, United States.
40. G. Martin, *Understanding Terrorism, Challenges, Perspectives and Issues*, Sage Publication, United States, 2003.
41. G. Stoudmann, 'Finding a Balance between Ensuring Security and Protecting Human Rights in the Fight against Terrorism' (2002) 13 (4) *Helsinki Monitor*.
42. H. Danelius, 'Convention against Torture and other Cruel, Inhumane or Degrading or Punishment' (2008) *United Nations Audiovisual Library of International Law*, http://untreaty.un.org/cod/avl/pdf/ha/catcidtp/catcidtp_e.pdf
43. H. J. Steiner et al, *International Human Rights in Context*, Oxford University Press, New York, 3rd Edition, 2007.
44. H.A Cooper, 'Terrorism: The Problem of Definition Revisited' (2001) 44 (6) *American Behavioural Scientist*.
45. Human Rights Watch, 'By the Numbers' 26 April 2006 http://www.hrw.org/node/11352/ section/2
46. Human Rights Watch, 'World Report 2003: United States' http://www.hrw.org/wr2k3/us.htmi
47. I. Cameron, 'General Human Rights Principles Relevant to US-EU Counter-terrorism Cooperation', in C. Fijnaut et al, *Legal Instruments in the Fight against International Terrorism,: A Transatlantic Dialogue*, 2004, Brill Academic Publishers.
48. I. Dobinson et al, Qualitative Legal Research, in M. McConville et al, *Research Methods for Law*, Edinburgh University Press, Edinburgh, 2007.
49. I. Duyvesteyn, The Role of History and Continuity in Terrorism Research, in M. Ranstrop (ed.), *Mapping Terrorism Research: State of the Art, Gaps and Future Direction*, Routledge, New York, 2007.
50. Inter-American Commission on Human Rights, Report on Terrorism and Human Rights, OEA/Ser.L/V/II.116Doc.5rev.1, 2002, Organization of American States, paragraph 53 http://www.ci   dh.org/terrorism/eng/part.a.htm#B.% 20International%20Human %20Rights %20Law
51. Inter-American Commission on Human Rights, Report on Terrorism and Human Rights, OEA/Ser.L/V/II.116Doc.5rev.1, 2002, Organization of American States, paragraph 55.
52. J. Donnelly, *Universal Human Rights in Theory and Practice*, Cornell University Press, United States, 2003.
53. J. Donnelly et al, 'Human Rights and the War on Terror', (2005), *Human Rights and Human Welfare Review Digest*, 1 http://www.du.edu/korbel/hrhw/ researchdigest terror/in dex.html
54. J. Ife, *Human Rights and Social Works: Towards Rights Based Practice*, Cambridge University Press, New York, 2001.
55. J. M. Lehmann, 'Limits to Counter-Terrorism: Comparing Derogation from the International Covenant on Civil and Political Rights and the European Convention on Human Rights', 104 http://projects.essex.ac.uk/ehrr/V8N1/Lehmann.pdf

56. J. Rehman, *Islamic State Practices, International Law and the Threat from Terrorism: A Critique of the'Clash of Civilizations' in the New World Order,* Hart Publishing, United States of America, 2005.

57. K.K. Koufa. 07 June 1999. Preliminary Report 18, 'Terrorism and Human Rights'. *United Nations Economic and Social Council, , Sub-Commission on Prevention of Discrimination and Protection. of Minorities.* UN. Doc. EICN.4/Sub.2/1999/27.

58. K. Watkin, 'Controlling the Use of Force: A Role for Human Rights Norms in Contemporary Armed Conflict', *The American Journal of International Law* 98(1).

59. Kofi Annan the United Nations Secretary General, 'Message on Human Rights Day', Department of Public Information, News and Media Division, New York, 10 December 2005.

60. L. A. Dickinson, 'Using legal process to fight terrorism: detentions, military commissions, international tribunals, and the rule of law' (2002) 75 *Southern California Law Review.*

61. L. Doswald-Beck, 'Fair Trial, Right to International Protection', Max Planck Encyclopedia of public International Law, paragraphs.

62. L. Doswald-Beck, *Fair Trial, Right to International Protection',* Max Planck *Encyclopedia of public International Law,* Oxford University Press, United Kingdom.

63. L. Doswald-Beck,'Fair Trial, Right to International Protection', Max Planck Encyclopedia of public International Law, *British Yearbook of International Law* 56 (1).

64. Lord Lester of Herne Hill, and David Pannick (Eds.), *Human Rights Law & Practice,* second edition, 2004, Butterworth, London.

65. M. Abrahms, The Causes of Terrorism: A Reappraisal of the Conventional Wisdom, Ph.D thesis, University of California, United States, 2009.

66. M. D. Filippo, 'Terrorist Crimes and International Co-operation: Critical Remarks on the Definition and Inclusion of Terrorism in the Category of International Crimes' (2008) 19 (3) *The European Journal of International Law (EJIL).*

67. M. D. Kielsgard, 'A Human Rights Approach to Counter-Terrorism', *California Western International Law Journal* 36(2).

68. M. Ignatieff, *Human Rights as Political and Idolatry,* Princeton University Press, 2001, United States.

69. M. Nowak, *CIA Extraordinary Rendition Flights, Torture and. Accountability: A European Approach,* 2008.

70. M. Satterthwaite, 'The US Program of Extraordinary Rendition and Secret Detention: Past and Future', in *CIA Extraordinary Rendition Flights, Torture and. Accountability: A European Approach,* European Centre for Constitutional and Human rights (ECCHR), Germany, 2008, 33 http://www.ecchr.de/index.php/ecchr-publications/articles/publications.html

71. M. Y. Omelicheva, Counter-terrorism and Human Rights: Explaining Differences in the Scope and Brutality of State's Responses to Terrorism, Ph.D thesis, Purdue University, United States, 2007.

72. M.L Volkansec et al, *Courts and Terrorism, Nine Nations Balance Rights and Security,* Cambridge University Press, New York, 2011.

73. N. Flowers, ' A Short History of Human Rights', University Minnesota, Human Rights   Resources   Centre

http://www1.umn.edu/humanrts/edumat/hreduseries/hereandnow/Part-1/short-history.htm
74. N.S. Jamwal, 'Counter Terrorism Strategy' (2003) 27(1) *Strategic Analysis.*
75. N.S. Saksena, *Terrorism, History and Facets in the World and in India*, Abhinav Publications, New Delhi, 1985.
76. O. Elagab et al, *International Law Documents Relating to Terrorism*, Cavendish, New York, 2007.
77. Office of the United Nations High Commissioner for Human Rights (OHCHR), 'Human Rights, Terrorism and Counter-Terrorism, Factsheet, No 32, http://www.ohchr.org/Documents/ Publications/Factsheet32EN.pdf
78. Organization for Security and Co-operation in Europe (OSCE), *Countering Terrorism, Protecting Human Rights: A Manual*, 2007, OSCE Office for Democratic Institutions and Human Rights (ODIHR), Poland, http://www.osce.org/odihr/29103
79. Organization for Security and Co-operation in Europe (OSCE), *Countering Terrorism, Protecting Human Rights: A Manual.*
80. Organization for Security and Co-operation in Europe (OSCE), The Bucharest Plan of Action for Combating Terrorism, 14 December 2001.http://www.UNCHR.org/refworld/docid/47fdfb250.html
81. P. Alston et al, 'The Competence of the UN Human Rights Council and its Special Procedures in relation to Armed Conflicts: Extrajudicial Executions in the War on Terror' (2008) 19 (1) *The European Journal of International Law (EJIL).*
82. P. Alston et al, 'The Competence of the UN Human Rights Council and its Special Procedures in relation to Armed Conflicts: Extrajudicial Executions in the War on Terror' (2008) 19 (1) *The European Journal of International Law (EJIL).*
83. P. G. Lauren, *The Evolution of International Human Rights*, University of Pennsylvania Press, Pennsylvania, 2011.
84. P. Hoffman, 'Human Rights and Terrorism' (2004) 26 *Human Rights Quarterly*, 941-942.
85. P. L. Griset et al, *'Terrorism in Perspective'*, Sage, London, 2003.
86. P. Morales, 'UNESCO's Philosophy of "intellectual and moral solidarity" in attaining peace', Paris: UNESCO, http://www.onlineunesco.org/UNESCO%27s%20Philosophy.html
87. P. N. Stearns, 'Why Study History?' (2008) *American Historical Association*, http://www.historians.org/pubs/free/WhyStudyHistory.htm
88. R. Young, 'Defining Terrorism: The Evolution of Terrorism as a Legal Concept in International Law and Its Influence on Definitions in Domestic Legislation' (2006) 29 (1) *Boston College International and Comparative Law Review.*
89. R. Law, *Terrorism: A History*, Polity Press, USA, 2009.
90. S. C. Stafford, 'Killing the Death Penalty with Kindness', in David R. Dow at al, *Machinary of Death*, 2002, Routledge, New York.
91. S. Cooper Blum 'Why and How of Preventive Detention in the War on Terror' (2009) 26 (1) *Thomas M. Cooley Law Review.*
92. S. Mahan et al, *Terrorism in perspective*, Sage, United States, 2003.
93. S. von Schorlemer, 'Human Rights: Substantive and Institutional Implications of the War against Terrorism' (2003) 14 (2) *European Journal of International Law (EJIL).*
94. Stanford Encyclopedia of Philosophy, 'Human Rights', 2003, http://plato.stanford.edu/ entries/rights-human

95. The Secretary General, All Must Work Together to Counter Terrorism, Prevent Spread of Weapons of Mass Destruction, Press Release, (06/03/2003), U.N. Doc. SG/SM/8624-SC/7680
http://www.un.org/News/Press/docs/2003/sgsm8624.doc.htm
96. The UN Secretary General Kofi Annan statement to the Security Council on 18 January 2002, accessible at: http://www.un.org/News/Press/docs/2002/sgsm8105.doc.htm
97. UN Commission on Human Rights, Report of the United Nations High Commissioner for Human Rights and Follow-up to the World Conference on Human Rights, E/CN.4/2002/18 Annex 2002, Economic and Social Council.
98. UN Commission on Human Rights, 27 February 2002, Report of the United Nations High Commissioner for Human Rights submitted pursuant to General Assembly resolution 48/141, 'Human Rights: A Uniting Framework', Economic and Social Council, http://www.unhchr.ch/Huridocda/Huridoca.nsf/0/817eec31cd2810f9c1256b87005 8a3e5/$FILE/G0211021.pdf
99. United Nations, Commission on Human Rights, Siracusa Principles on the Limitation and Derogation Provisions in the International Covenant on Civil and Political Rights, E/CN.4, 1985, paragraph 158 http://www.cidh.org/terrorism/eng/part.a.htm#B.20International%20 Human%20Rights %20Law
100.   United Nations, Human Rights Committee, General Comment No 6 (1982) The Right to Life, (art. 6): 04/30/1982.CCPR.http://www.unhchr.ch/tbs/doc.nsf/0/84ab9690ccd81fc 7c12563ed0046fae3
101.   United Nations, Peace and Security Section of the Department of Public Information, 'United Nations Counter-Terrorism Strategy Background Notes', 2009, http://www.un.org/terrorism/pdfs/CT_Back ground_March_2009_terrorism2.pdf
102.   W. Laqueur, *The New Terrorism: Fanaticism and the Arms of Mass Destruction*, 1999, Oxford University Press, New York.
103.   W. Laqueur, *A History of Terrorism*, 2001, New Jersey, Transaction Publishers.
104.   W. F. Shughart II, 'An analytical history of terrorism 1945-2000' (2006) 128 (1-2) *Public Choice*.

www.ingramcontent.com/pod-product-compliance
Lightning Source LLC
Chambersburg PA
CBHW032025170526
45157CB00002B/858